the complete
HOME
AQUARIUM

the complete
HOME
AQUARIUM

by Hans J. Mayland
Translated and adapted by Gwynne Vevers
Consultant editor, Michael Oliver

Grosset & Dunlap Publishers New York

Contents

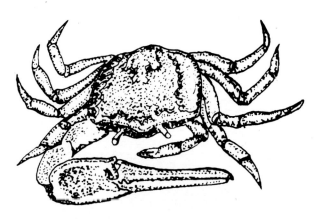

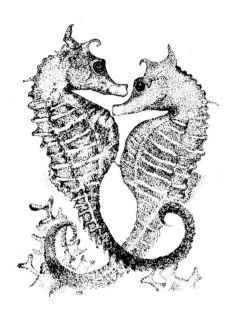

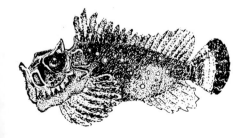

First published in the United States in 1976
by Grosset & Dunlap, Inc., 51 Madison Avenue,
New York, New York 10010

© 1975 by Falken-Verlag Erich Sicker KG, West Germany
English translation © 1976 by Ward Lock Limited, London
All rights reserved
Library of Congress catalog card number: 76-20307
ISBN 0 448 12708 3
Reprinted 1978

Published in Great Britain by Ward Lock Limited, London,
a member of the Pentos Group

Printed in Singapore

Preface

Over seventy per cent of the earth's surface is covered with water, most of it sea water. It is, therefore, only right that man should take an interest in the living things that inhabit this aquatic environment. His original interest in fishes and other aquatic animals was primarily as a source of food, and this still continues. In more recent times, however, a considerable amount of attention has been devoted to the study of aquatic animals that have no economic importance, and in so doing various highly sophisticated methods of keeping them in aquaria have been worked out. In fact, the development of the aquarium, whether public or private, dates back only to the middle of the 19th century. Progress since then has been rapid and the range of fishes and invertebrates kept in aquaria is now immense.

In his very attractive book Hans Mayland has gathered together an impressive selection of freshwater and marine fishes and has given a lively text describing how they are best kept in the aquarium. His colour illustrations show quite clearly that some fishes are among the most brightly coloured of all animals, equalling and even surpassing many tropical butterflies and birds in brilliance.

The first part of the book is just as important, for it provides a clear account of the techniques used in aquarium work, and this will allow the beginner aquarist to grasp the essentials of filtration, heating, lighting, pH, water quality and so on.

Finally, as a working biologist I particularly like the way in which Hans Mayland has drawn on his own practical experience at home and also in parts of the tropics to explain the biological background to the aquarium. The result is a useful account of the cycle of events in natural waters. This will enable the reader to understand the vastly complicated, but endlessly fascinating interrelationships of plants, fishes, and other animals living in the seas, lakes and rivers of the world.

Gwynne Vevers
March, 1976

7

PART ONE
The Freshwater Aquarium

Introduction

The natural environment of aquarium fishes

Aquarium fishes come from all five continents, though the majority come from tropical waters which, in spite of their closeness to the equator, offer very varied living conditions. This is primarily due to the nature of the rocks over which the rivers flow. When the rocks are rich in minerals the water will be hard, but if they are poor in minerals the water will remain soft. In most cases rivers arise in upland areas. They owe their origin to precipitation in the form of rain or snow, which is produced by evaporation. Such waters are soft, since any mineral salts originally dissolved in them are not evaporated and remain in the ground.

Thus all waters are originally soft, unless they have come from a deep well. The greatest reservoir of fresh water in the world, the Amazon basin in South America, receives water from tributaries in the surrounding areas of mountain: the highlands of Guyana in the north, the Cordillera chain in the west and the highlands of the Mato Grosso in the south. The country through which all these rivers flow is very deficient in minerals, and the waters of the Amazon basin are in fact the softest known. The fishes living in them are adapted to this type of water.

In Africa, on the other hand, the waters are quite different, apart from the Zaïre (Congo) basin from which relatively few aquarium fishes are imported. All the other collecting areas in Africa show varying degrees of water hardness.

On the west coast these fishes come from areas near the coast, where sea water with its high mineral content sometimes penetrates far into the rivers. Other aquarium fishes come from East Africa, including the rift-valley area. There the numerous lakes all have hard water. These lakes are the home of many attractive cichlids which have evolved over the course of thousands of years, so that there are now large numbers of species which have become adapted to living in every available ecological niche. Thus, there are fishes which can live and breed in the soda lakes of Kenya and Tanzania at temperatures above 40°C (104°F) and in spite of the extremely high mineral content; thousands of tons of pure soda are removed commercially every year from this area. It is evident therefore that fishes are hardy animals which have the ability to adapt to unfavourable conditions. It is essential, however, to realize that the process of adaptation is a slow one, taking very long periods of time, which are perhaps difficult to contemplate.

Water hardness and the content of various dissolved substances are not the only factors which affect the life of aquarium fishes. The water is only one factor in the total environment. Not all parts of a river or lake provide the same conditions. In some parts the bottom may be sandy, in others rocky. Some waters flow fast, others slowly or not at all. So there may be several different habitats in a single river or lake, each containing suitably adapted fishes and other aquatic animals. Such adaptations to environmental conditions may involve body form, feeding methods, respiration, reproduction and behaviour. Thus the lengthy process of biological evolution has produced peaceful and predatory species; fishes that swim fast and those that lurk on the bottom; fishes that are brightly coloured and those that appear drab, and so on. The aquarist must, therefore, provide conditions to suit fishes from different habitats, and he must know which species can be kept together and which must be kept apart. The section dealing with the individual families and species of fishes will provide information on all these aspects.

The aquarium fishes on sale to the public come from a variety of sources. As a rule the more expensive species will have been imported. These are usually species which cannot be bred and have to be transported over long distances from their home waters. The long journey is itself a test of the health of the fishes. For example, the neon tetras and the various armoured catfishes caught in the area of the upper Rio Negro are placed in large plastic containers, fitted with continuous water circulation, and transported in covered boats, over a period of a week or more to Manaus, where the Amazon and Rio Negro unite. Here the fishes are re-packed in plastic bags which are placed in insulated cartons and then flown to all parts of the world. When they finally reach the aquarists' tanks they have already travelled more than most of us do in a lifetime.

Fishes that are more reasonably priced have almost certainly been bred in captivity, but this is no disadvantage. On the contrary, these are often the species with a robust constitution, which has enabled them to breed under conditions different from those experienced by their ancestors in the wild. They are often not so fastidious about the quality of the water, and they have to some extent become domesticated.

Certain points should be kept in mind when buying aquarium fishes. A fish must be healthy and feeding properly. First, one should check the body form and compare it with that of other members of the same species. Fishes that show abnormal curvature or irregular swimming movements or which lurk in a corner of the tank should not be bought. They may be suffering from some disease or internal injury, or they may have genetic defects. A healthy fish should have a smooth skin, free of any small white spots or excrescences and without areas of blood-shot tissue.

Fishes bought from a dealer who has put them in a plastic bag should be taken without delay to the aquarist's home. The plastic bag is certainly a great boon, but it is only for use as a temporary container, as the oxygen in the bag will quickly be used up. The temperature of the water in the plastic bag should be compared as soon as possible with that of the water in the aquarium tank. If there is a difference between the two temperatures, the bag should merely be floated on the surface of the tank. After one or two hours the temperatures should be the same, and the bag can then be carefully emptied into the tank. The fishes must now be given a period of rest so that they can explore their new surroundings and perhaps look for suitable hiding-places. In most cases, it is only after this that the fishes will show their full coloration and start to feed. Care should of course be taken to ensure that newly purchased fishes are put into a tank where the water is suitable for their requirements.

Aquarium tanks and equipment

Creating an aquatic environment

Tanks for aquarium plants and animals can be of various sizes and made from a wide variety of materials. In general, the length of the tank should be greater than its height, and it should be so constructed that only one side is transparent. The back wall should be used for decorative purposes. Tanks having the width more or less the same as the height should only be used for breeding fishes such as angelfishes which have tall fins. For a normal tank the ratio of length:width:height should be 10:5:6 or 10:3:4.

Just as the water content of the tank is restricted so also must be the number of fishes and plants accommodated in it. The number of fishes that can be put into a tank is usually given as the volume of water (in litres) required for each specimen. At one time it was said that each fish up to 5 cm (2 in) in length required a volume of 2 litres ($3\frac{1}{2}$ pints) of water, but this is certainly not enough. Beginners in the aquarium hobby often lose sight of the fact that their fishes will grow if the conditions are suitable. It is much better to buy young specimens and grow them on in your own tank. After a few months they should have grown quite considerably.

It is best to allow 2 litres ($3\frac{1}{2}$ pints) of water for each centimetre ($\frac{1}{3}$ in) of fish, provided the maximum height of the fish does not exceed 2 cm ($\frac{3}{4}$ in).

Example 1: a tank measuring $100 \times 30 \times 40$ cm (c. $40 \times 12 \times 16$ in) has a capacity of 120 litres (26 gallons). From this 20 litres (c. $4\frac{1}{2}$ gallons) should be subtracted to allow for sand, gravel and rocks, leaving 100 litres (22 gallons) of water. If the fishes are each about 6 cm ($2\frac{1}{4}$ in) long and not above 2 cm ($\frac{3}{4}$ in) tall, then each one will require 9–12 litres (2–$2\frac{3}{4}$ gallons) of water, so the tank can support 8 to 10 fishes.

Example 2: a tank measuring $80 \times 26 \times 38$ cm (c. $32 \times 10 \times 15$ in) has a capacity of 79 litres (17 gallons), from which 14 litres (3 gallons) should be subtracted to allow for the volume of the decorative material, thus leaving 65 litres (14 gallons). Assuming that the aquarist intends to buy young neon tetras each 2 cm ($\frac{3}{4}$ in) long, then each one would require 4 litres (0.9 gallon) and the tank could be stocked with 65 divided by 4 = 16 fishes. This would not, however, be advisable because after a few months the fishes will have reached their maximum length of 4 cm ($1\frac{1}{2}$ in), so each would then require 8 litres (1.8 gallons) and the tank would be grossly overcrowded. The aquarist would, in fact, be better advised to start with not more than 10 to 12 fishes to allow for growth, and also for a few deaths.

Such examples are only intended to be a rough guide. The important point to realize is that life in an aquarium tank is not static, for changes are taking place continually. As time goes on the processes of growth and death will alter the general appearance of the tank, but these are natural phenomena and should result in what can be called a well-established tank with healthy inmates.

Tank types

Tanks constructed of welded angle-iron, with a bottom of metal or wired glass and panes of glass held in with mastic are gradually becoming outmoded. This is largely because they have been found to be less practical than more modern types. For example, the frame of a tank can now be made of anodized aluminium and the glass panes bonded with silicone rubber. There are

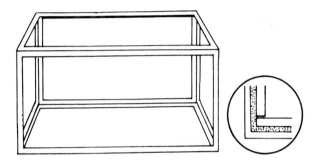

Diagram to show the structure of an angle-iron tank

also tanks which have metal framing round the upper and lower edges only, the vertical joints being made with a silicone glue. The latter material is excellent for aquarium purposes.

Tanks can also be made of glass panes sealed with silicone glue alone, but here the glass itself must be somewhat thicker. Naturally, with a tank in which the panes are glued together, the quality of the workmanship is of prime importance. Whether the aquarist makes the tank himself or buys it from a dealer, the durability of the final product will depend on the quality of the materials used, as well as on the care with which they have been assembled. It is worth mentioning that silicone rubbers are not all the same. The hardening system is important for the final strength of the job, but the nature of the original solvent is important. Some use chemicals, such as phenol, which may release toxic substances, but it is quite safe to use a silicone-rubber glue in which the solvent is acetic acid, immediately recognizable because it smells of vinegar. Bostik 1581 Silicone Sealant has never caused any problems. Before using a silicone glue it is essential to ensure that the glass is completely free of grease or oil. New panes are often given a thin protective coating of grease, and this must be removed by using acetone. Unlike most glues which harden with heat, the hardening of silicone rubber depends upon humidity, and on average the process takes about twenty-four hours.

Plastic tanks are attractive in appearance. The material can be bent and jointed, and a tank made from it is just as durable as any other. For aquarium purposes plastic is, in fact, just as good as glass and it does not scratch unless roughly handled. Some modern plastic tanks look as though they consist of only one piece. The material is produced in more than one colour and this allows the rear wall, for instance, to be of a different colour, a point which may well be useful when deciding on the decoration of a tank.

Asbestos-cement tanks have become popular in recent years partly because of the increased interest in marine aquarium keeping. These tanks are heavy and have only one glass pane. They cannot, of course, corrode, which is an important point when sea water is being used.

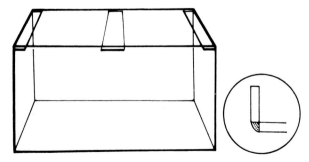

An all-glass tank, with the panes of glass glued together with a silicone-rubber compound

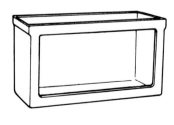

Diagram showing an asbestos-cement tank

Decorative rockwork can be attached to the rear wall and this improves the appearance of the tank when filled with water and fishes. The asbestos-cement sheets are manufactured under pressure, and they can be cut with a saw, but it is more convenient to buy the sheets ready cut from a dealer. The material may give off undesirable substances into the aquarium water, so all the internal surfaces must be sealed. The best preparation for this is an epoxy resin, of the type sold as two components which are mixed immediately before use. The mixture hardens very rapidly. Provided the tank is absolutely dry before the resin is applied, the result should be extremely durable.

All-glass tanks cast in one piece can be used for special purposes. Tanks of this type measuring about $36 \times 26 \times 24$ cm (c. $14 \times 10 \times 9$ in) with a capacity of 20 litres (c. $4\frac{1}{2}$ gallons) would be quite useful for breeding. For this purpose they have the advantage that they are easy to keep clean. They are, however, very likely to crack and are then quite useless as they cannot be repaired. Furthermore the glass, being cast, is difficult to see through. On the whole, all-glass tanks are rapidly becoming obsolete for aquarium work. Similar small tanks can also be made out of plastic, and these are much lighter and handier to use.

Some aquarists like to have fish tanks built into cupboards, bookcases or other items of household furniture. These are constructed as complete units with their own heating and lighting, and with a removable cover for servicing. Nowadays, furniture used for this purpose is usually made of timber with a plastic veneer. When this is done it is quite essential that there should be adequate ventilation to prevent condensation building up in the cupboard and seeping into the timber. Care should be taken to seal all the timber joints.

A fitted aquarium of this type can be made to look very attractive, but it also has the advantage that it forms a self-contained unit, as all the equipment and accessories, including an air pump and filters, can be stored in it.

Tank weights and positioning

These two subjects are closely related. The larger an aquarium tank the greater its weight, so one has to consider its position in the room. First, one should find out the actual weight of the tank when full, and relate this to the structure and strength of the flooring. This is a point which may be forgotten in the excitement of acquiring a new aquarium. A tank measuring $80 \times 26 \times 38$ cm (c. $32 \times 10 \times 15$ in) holds about 80 litres (c. 18 gallons) of water and this weighs 80 kg (176 lb). To this one must add the weight of the tank when empty and of its stand. The total would not be much different from the weight of a man. If, however, the length of the tank is increased by only 20 cm (8 in), and the other dimensions in proportion, giving a tank measuring $100 \times 40 \times 50$ cm ($40 \times 16 \times 20$ in) then the capacity will be 200 litres (44 gallons), weighing 200 kg (440 lb). This is an increase in weight of over 150%, and of course the weight of the empty tank will also have increased.

The most suitable place for positioning a heavy object is close to one of the walls of a room, where the bearing capacity is considerably greater than it is in the centre. Thanks to the efficiency of modern lighting there is no need to position the tank close to one of the windows. In fact this would lead to an unattractive growth of algae on one side of the tank, due to excess light. It is much better to place the tank in a darker corner and to use lighting which can be properly controlled. An aquarium tank requires light for the whole of the day if all the natural biological processes are to proceed as they should. It is no use coming home from work and switching on the light. Aquarium plants and fishes are adapted to living in tropical sunlight, and anyone who is unwilling to provide the modern substitute of electric light would be well advised to give up the idea of keeping an aquarium and turn to other interests.

Making one's own tank

The construction of an aquarium tank should be attempted only by those with a practical bent who are used to working to exact standards. A slight fault in construction may have serious consequences. Normally proportioned tanks, such as those discussed above, can be obtained through ordinary trade channels. Special sizes can be made to order, and on the whole it is better to get this done by a firm of specialists.

Technical equipment

Filters, which help to keep the aquarium water clean, are of various types: internal or external, fast or slow. Many aquarists are primarily concerned with the optical clarity of the water, but this is not the whole story. Small amounts of visible detritus are not necessarily deleterious, whereas small amounts of invisible dissolved substances may cause serious trouble. Impurities in the water come from the faeces of the fishes and from the unconsumed remains of their food. At one time small filters were suspended on the outside of the aquarium tank, but certain modern types are more efficient.

The rivers, streams and lakes from which aquarium fishes come are still unpolluted, and they can be said to be self-cleaning. In an aquarium the amount of water per fish is relatively small and so it becomes polluted more rapidly. Even with ideal lighting and vegetation there will be no chance that the organic and inorganic waste products will be fully broken down so that the water returns to its original state. The use of a suitable filter does, however, help in the process of purifying the water.

In order to avoid any misunderstanding it should be stated clearly that no filter can bring the water back to its original state, for the water is undergoing changes the whole time. It has, for example, to be warmed, usually to 24–26°C (75–79°F), for the successful maintenance of tropical aquarium fishes. This increases the rate of evaporation, but remember that only the water evaporates. The mineral substances dissolved in it do not evaporate but remain in the tank water. If the tank is then topped up with ordinary fresh water this will add more dissolved material. In this way the water becomes increasingly 'dense', because with time the introduced substances become more concentrated. Among the substances involved is calcium, and as it becomes more concentrated the water becomes harder. A hardness testing kit will show how rapidly this happens in an aquarium tank.

How then can we prevent the water becoming harder? Warm water evaporates more rapidly than cold. Many fishes are kept at too high a temperature. The heating unit should never be set higher than is necessary. This would increase the rate of evaporation. In addition, it is an advantage to fill the tank with water that is poor in mineral salts, perhaps with de-ionized water. This applies particularly in areas where the mains water has a hardness of over 20° DH. If this method proves too expensive, then it is not sufficient just to replace the water that has evaporated; rather, part of the water should be renewed. Partial renewal is better for the animals and plants than a renewal of all the water. The latter would entail too rapid a change, so it is much better to carry out several small renewals at frequent intervals.

At one time aquarists dreamt and talked about the possibility of achieving a perfect natural equilibrium between animals, plants and water, but this almost never happens. It would need a very large tank with masses of plants and rather few fishes, and this would scarcely suit the modern aquarist.

Tank water can, however, be kept in good condition by various means, and one of the most important of these is filtration. As already mentioned, there are two principal types of filter: the internal and the external, which may be either fast or slow.

Internal filters

As the name implies these are set up inside the aquarium tank, and they are therefore visible, a point which many aquarists do not like. The slow internal filter is a transparent plastic container filled with a suitable medium, fixed in a corner of the tank, and fitted with an air-lift (see p. 21, aeration). This type of filter has the disadvantage that all the detritus swirling around in the water gets sucked in, so that the

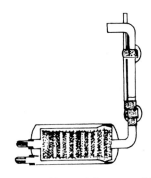

Internal filter with renewable cartridge

filter medium becomes clogged. An internal filter with a cartridge is perhaps more efficient; this can be attached to the glass by suckers and is worked by an air-lift. When this becomes clogged the foam plastic cartridge is quickly renewed (see fig. p. 15). A slow bottom filter is also fitted internally, but there are also methods of using bottom filtration powered by an external motor to give fast filtration; this is the Eheim system (see diagrams on this page).

Here it is appropriate to discuss briefly whether or not it is advantageous to have a continuous flow of water through the gravel or sand, known technically as the substrate. In an ordinary tank the substrate does not have a constant flow of water passing through and so it does not receive oxygen. If the bottom is used as a filter then oxygen will reach it and aerobic bacteria can settle there. A substrate that is deficient in oxygen, on the other hand, will only have anaerobic bacteria, which produce metabolic products that foul the water and create an evil smell. These products are usually poisonous to fishes and plants. On the other hand, aerobic bacteria living in the substrate fulfill a useful purpose, for they convert metabolic products into substances that are biologically harmless. Opponents of the bottom filter point out that it removes nutrient substances, but this is not a very serious objection.

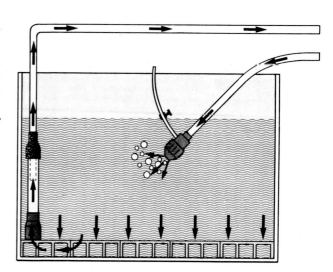

Substrate filtration with the water moving downwards through the substrate

Two systems of bottom substrate filtration may be mentioned: one involves the slow flow of water from below upwards (see fig. below left), the other having a rapid flow from above downwards (see fig. above). In the first method the connecting inlet tube (on left in diagram) leads to a shallow box on the bottom which has numerous slits. Water is pushed by an external motor down through the connecting tube and is distributed around the substrate which lies above the box. In this way the substrate acts as a filter. The speed of flow can be regulated by a tap outside the tank. The substrate itself must not of course be too fine or it will become clogged.

For rapid filtration flowing from above downwards, the connecting tube (on the left of the diagram above) must be connected with the suction end of the motor, so that the tank water is sucked down through the substrate which again acts as a filter. The substrate must consist of coarse particles (5 mm ($\frac{1}{5}$ in) or more in diameter) to prevent fine particles of detritus from settling and clogging the bottom. In addition, the motor must be fairly powerful. This type of filtration is not suitable for a planted aquarium tank, but is excellent for keeping larger cichlids in tanks without plants.

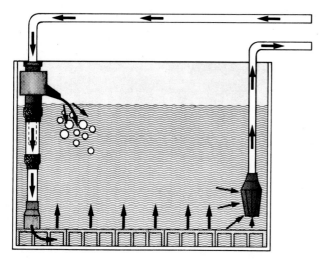

Substrate filtration with the water moving upwards through the substrate

Rapid filtration can also be carried out by using a motor-driven internal filter with a centrifugal pump (see diagram, p. 17). This has been used mainly for the marine aquarium, but it is also suitable for freshwater tanks, particularly those containing fishes that dig (e.g. cichlids) and with few or no plants. These pumps produce rapid water movements, which suit fishes such as certain loaches, which come from fast-flowing rivers. In some models the flow can be reduced. The only disadvantage is that the rapid movement of the water very soon brings all the detritus onto the filter medium, so that the container soon becomes clogged and no longer allows sufficient water to pass through. The pump will then stop unless the filter is thoroughly cleaned, a job which may be time-consuming.

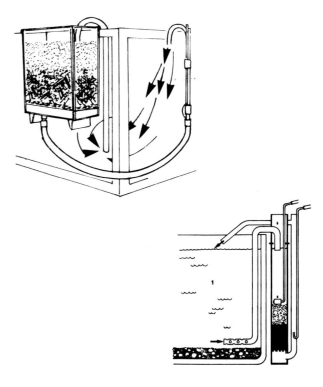

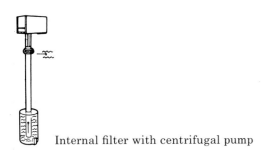

Internal filter with centrifugal pump

External filter worked by an air-lift shown on the extreme right of the lower diagram

External filters

These are much used for freshwater tanks. They are not only efficient but they also have the advantage that all the technical equipment is out of sight, so that the tank is more aesthetically pleasing. The only item visible is the tube carrying the water from the tank to the filter.

Here again, one can distinguish between slow and fast filters. For a slow external filter the water is taken from the tank to the filter by an air-lift. By this method up to 200 litres (44 gallons) of water can be moved per hour. The external filter itself usually consists of a rectangular plastic container, open at the top, which is filled with the filter medium. The water flows from the aquarium into the top of the filter, passes down through the filter medium, and is returned to the aquarium tank by an air-lift.

The use of a motor-driven external filter is be-

An Eheim motorized filter

coming more widespread. The different models of the Eheim combined pump and filter are designed for various tank sizes with the appropriate pumping capacity and volume of filter medium. Here the flow of the water is reversed, for it is led into the filter from below and passes upwards through the medium with the help of the pump (see diagram p. 17). This system has two main advantages: 1) it is clean in operation and the filter medium, held in bags, is easily renewed, and 2) the inlet and outlet tubes allow the insertion of other equipment, such as an ultra-violet tube for destroying micro-organisms. The only disadvantage is that it uses rather a lot of electric current.

On balance the Eheim system is very efficient, but it is quite essential that the filter medium should be changed at regular intervals, and perhaps more frequently than the manufacturers recommend. Some aquarists suggest that the filter medium should be changed every two weeks. If this is not done the water may appear to be relatively clean to the naked eye, but in practice the filter medium will have become clogged with waste, and will be continually shedding poisonous impurities into the water that is going back into the aquarium tank.

In spite of this invisible pollution the filtering part of an Eheim does not become so clogged that the water flow is stopped. The filter medium is usually packed in bags of nylon which are pervious to water.

Several different materials can be used for the filter, as for instance sand, gravel, nylon wool, activated charcoal, peat or certain new synthetic resins. Sand and gravel are very good for filtration, particularly when the two are used together, e.g. coarse gravel/finer gravel/sand, a combination which efficiently retains fine particles of detritus. The different sizes of particle prevent the whole mass from becoming too closely packed. Such a mixture is, however, heavy and difficult to handle, so nowadays nylon wool is usually used for catching the very fine particles. This material is light in weight and extremely easy to clean. On no account should glass wool be used in a filter, as tiny pieces break off and find their way into the aquarium, where they may cause injury and death to the fishes.

When activated charcoal is used for aquarium filtration the water should first be passed through a layer of nylon wool in order to remove the coarse particles of detritus and other undesirable material. This is done because the activated charcoal has a structure of very fine pores which quickly become clogged by coarse particles. The water must, therefore, have been subjected to mechanical prefiltration, otherwise the charcoal will quickly become useless. The nylon wool will only hold back a certain amount of waste material, so it must be cleaned regularly. Activated charcoal will absorb only albuminous waste, but not ammonia in solution which is poisonous to fishes, or the dissolved nitrites and nitrates that accumulate in aquarium water. If, as already mentioned, the charcoal is not renewed very frequently the filter will be removing visible waste but doing nothing else. The albuminous substances absorbed by the charcoal will start to break down into ammonia and other poisonous substances.

Filtration through peat is also a very suitable method of treatment for most aquarium waters. It can have a most beneficial effect on life in the tank, but this will depend upon its quality, for not all peats are the same. One of the varying factors is the content of so-called humic acids,

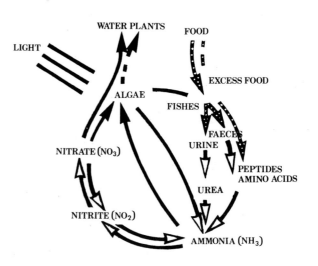

Diagram to show the nitrogen cycle:
Nitrite is a nitrogen compound which is formed in the aquarium by the breakdown of organic substances, such as fish faeces, urine, food remains and the dead parts of plants. Nitrite is only one of the stages in the breakdown of organic nitrogen to inorganic nitrate

and this depends upon its place of origin. It is widely but erroneously believed that all peat is acid, but this is not so. However, an acid peat is the one to use in the aquarium. Nowadays, horticultural suppliers sell 'improved' peats which are enriched with various fertilizers, but these must not be used for aquarium purposes. Aquarist suppliers normally stock suitable acid peats.

In addition to its content of humic acids and its ability to lower the pH of the water (acidification), peat also contains hormone-like substances, which are known, for example, to encourage the growth of young plants and of various delicate plants such as orchids. Peat imparts a brownish colour to the water.

In a well-kept aquarium tank the correct numbers of beneficial bacteria do a continuous job of breaking down and converting organic waste materials. On the other hand, badly kept tanks, with an excess of waste matter, become breeding grounds for enormous numbers of injurious bacteria. This leads to clouding of the water, due to the multiplication of single-celled protozoans, which feed on the bacteria. This state of affairs is not good for either plants or fishes, and indeed some aquarium fishes, such as cardinal tetras and discus fishes, which are difficult to breed, are known to be particularly sensitive to the presence of bacteria. This problem can be largely solved by filtration through peat, which reduces the load of micro-organisms.

After a certain time peat loses its beneficial properties and it must then be renewed. In general, it is best to renew a peat filter every three to four weeks, and at the same time to replace a proportion of the water.

Heating

Although a few cold-water fishes are kept by some home aquarists, the vast majority of aquarium fishes come from the tropics, and so their tank water must be kept warm. In their home ranges the water is kept warm by the sun's energy and is usually in the region of 22–26°C (72–79°F), rising sometimes to 30°C (86°F). These are the approximate temperatures at which aquarium water should be kept, although during the winter months (November to February) some tropical fishes can easily tolerate a drop of

a few degrees. During this period cold-water fishes should be kept, if possible, at a temperature of 10–14°C (50–57°F).

A tropical aquarium should not be subject to sudden variations in temperature, and so it should never be installed in a place where this can occur, e.g. in a draughty corridor, or close to a radiator. A sudden drop in temperature has an inhibiting effect on metabolism and on the blood circulation, and it reduces resistance to disease. This is why a complete change of the water in a tank may be so injurious to the fishes and also to the plants. Reduced temperatures often affect the functioning of the swimbladder, and this results in abnormal swimming.

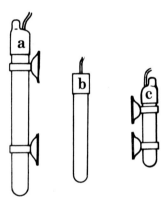

a) heater with thermostat
b) heater without thermostat
c) thermostat without the heater

Nowadays the electric heaters used in aquarium tanks work on the same principle as an immersion heater. The wattage of the heater should be roughly the same as the volume of water to be heated, i.e. 100 watts for 100 litres (22 gallons).

There are two types of heater: the ordinary aquarium heater (fig. b, above) which can be controlled by a separate thermostat (fig. c) and the combined heater and thermostat (fig. a, above). For small tanks there is no doubt that the latter should be used. For larger tanks (length over 100 cm or 40 in) it is better to install the necessary number of heaters, and to have these controlled by a single thermostat. The filter will help to keep the water moving so that the heat is dispersed. The operative part of the heater is a wire element wound round an insulated tube, which is sealed into an outer glass casing.

It is quite essential that the heater itself should not be buried in the substrate, nor touching the tank glass. Most types of heater can be fixed to the glass by suction cups. The thermostat is set at a given temperature and being coupled to the heater it then keeps the water at this temperature. In other words the thermostat turns the heater off and on automatically.

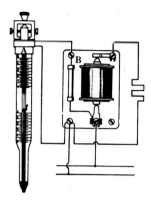

Contact thermometer (a) which, through a relay (b), switches the heaters on or off

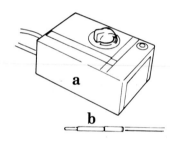

Thermostatically controlled switch gear (a); with a separate probe (b)

There is also thermostatically controlled switch equipment (diagram above), which is particularly useful for breeding, where there is a series of tanks of the same size each with its own heater, but all controlled by a single thermostat.

Another method of maintaining an exact temperature is to use a contact thermometer and relay (above right). The thermometer part consists of a long glass tube, in which there are two thermometers, one (above) for the desired temperature and one (below) for the actual temperature in the tank. This is connected to a relay which activates the switch, keeping the water temperature exactly at the desired setting.

Unless the aquarist is a skilled electrician he should on no account attempt to assemble his aquarium heating equipment. To do so would not only be probably more expensive but would certainly be highly dangerous. Aquarium dealers stock numerous types of heaters and these are usually well made and reliable.

Circulation and aeration

Many aquarium owners value aeration rather too highly. It has a useful function but it would be wrong to think that every air bubble releases oxygen into the water. In most cases aeration certainly helps to circulate the water, but it is not very efficient at increasing the oxygen content. In general, aeration is not so important in a freshwater tank as it is in a marine one, where the fishes, and particularly the invertebrates, need it.

In any aquarium tank oxygen enters the water at its surface, and obviously the greater the surface area the more oxygen can be absorbed. This is on the assumption that the surface is clean, but this is not always so. Occasionally a tank develops a thin surface layer of dust and oil and this prevents the interchange of gases (oxygen and carbon dioxide). This slightly iridescent layer is also dangerous to surface-living fishes, and it must be removed by drawing tissue paper across it.

The two main constituents of air are oxygen and nitrogen, and for aquarium purposes it is the oxygen which is of primary importance. Perhaps fortunately for our present purpose water absorbs oxygen more readily than nitrogen, so that the air dissolved in water is relatively richer in oxygen than atmospheric air. In addition, the oxygen content is higher in cool water, in moving waters and in waters rich in vegetation. Oxygen escapes rapidly from heated tank water. The rate of respiration of the fishes then increases as they attempt to get more oxygen, and eventually they come to the surface and try to gulp air. At the same time the fishes will be producing carbon dioxide, which will further worsen the situation. At this point it would be possible to take out a proportion of the water and replace it with new water at the same temperature. Alternatively, the aquarist can use an aerator which will effectively move the water round so that the surface changes the whole time and oxygen enters. As already mentioned, this is perhaps the main function of aeration, for not much of the oxygen in the air bubbles is actually released into the water.

One of the simplest methods of aeration is to use a small diaphragm pump, which propels air through a length of tubing and releases it into the water as a stream of bubbles. By using a diffuser stone the bubbles will be much finer.

These pumps work on a relatively simple principle: an electro-magnet starts a diaphragm vibrating and this sucks in air, which passes through an aperture to the delivery tube. The pump must have sufficient power to overcome the resistance caused by the water pressure in the tank. Some resistance is also built up by the fine pore structure of the diffuser stone. The aeration produced by such a pump is normally sufficient for most fishes.

There is a disadvantage in this method of aeration which is more serious in marine than in freshwater tanks. The bubbles of air are released in very large numbers, and most of these rise directly to the surface and produce a spray, which settles on the tank cover and on the lamps. In a marine tank the water part of the spray will evaporate, leaving a crust consisting of a mixture of salts, and this builds up quite rapidly. Even in a freshwater tank the spray will contain some calcium and this will appear as an opaque greyish film.

An alternative method is to use a diaphragm pump to operate an air-lift. The principle is quite simple. A glass or rigid plastic tube is positioned vertically in the water so that its bottom end is about an inch above the substrate, while its top end protrudes about an inch or so above the water surface and is bent over at an angle. Air from the vibrator pump is led into

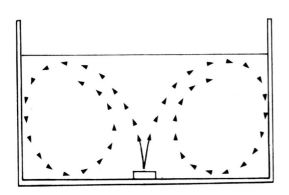

A diffuser stone is primarily intended to set up turbulence in the water

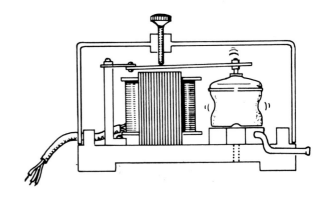

Diagram showing the structure of a diaphragm pump

the bottom of the tube and as the bubbles rise they carry water with them, so that a mixture of air and water reaches the top where it is expelled. This mixture can either fall back into the aquarium tank directly or it can fall onto an external filter. In either case the water will have been enriched with oxygen.

If the pump has to be switched off for some reason, there is always a chance that as the pump pressure drops water will be sucked back up the delivery tube and possibly into the pump itself, and this will obviously cause damage. To prevent this happening it is best to position the pump well above the tank.

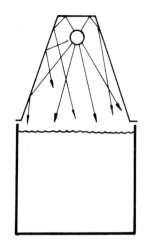

Lighting

Light is an essential factor in the life of practically all living organisms. The artificial lighting used for an aquarium must take account of the tank size and of the light conditions in the room in which it stands.

The light requirements of fishes and water plants vary considerably, and in the wild there are of course daily and seasonal fluctuations in light. Some plants and fishes like plenty of sunlight, others need less, and certain fish species prefer a certain time of day for spawning. Strong sunlight over a prolonged period may cause trouble in an aquarium tank with plants, as the latter may produce so much oxygen that the water becomes saturated. Under such conditions the fishes will suffer. Factors such as this should be taken into account when choosing a position for the tank.

In nature, fishes and other aquatic organisms always receive light from above. In a home aquarium, on the other hand, light can enter from all four sides as well as from above. It is therefore not advisable to position the tank close to a window which may from time to time receive bright sunlight. It is much better to have the aquarium elsewhere in the room, possibly in a dark corner, and to illuminate it with artificial lighting which is controllable. Thus an aquarium tank becomes independent of the seasonal changes of light found in temperate regions.

Fortunately for the aquarium world, the lighting industry now produces a wide range of very suitable equipment. The introduction of fluorescent lighting solved the problem of finding a

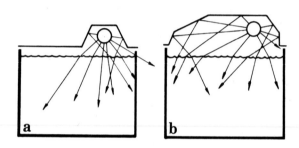

With the reflector positioned high up above the tank the light rays will be approximately parallel. If the reflector is too small (a) the lamp will only illuminate the tank area immediately below it. With a good reflector (b) all parts of the tank will be illuminated

bright light source in a shallow fitting. It only remains to choose the best type of fluorescent lighting, and here the requirements of the aquarium plants are of primary importance. The assimilation process of plants, or photosynthesis, is mainly dependent upon the blue and the red parts of the spectrum. Special fluorescent tubes have been developed which produce this type of light, e.g. Osram Fluora and Sylvania Gro-lux. The mixture of red and blue rays emitted by these lamps stimulates plant growth.

Aquarium lighting can be said to have three main functions. First, it must encourage plant growth; secondly it must bring out the colours of the fishes, and thirdly it must not encourage too much algal growth. Naturally, the amount of light used in a freshwater tank depends upon the species of plants and animals being kept.

The suggestions given in the table on this page are intended to act as guide-lines.

By installing switch equipment it is possible to switch each lamp on and off at will, and thus to vary the amount of light. It is possible to have too much light, and this may lead to excessive growth of algae. A small amount of green algae on the rocks is quite normal and it supplies extra food for some fishes, and for snails. On the other hand, brown or beige-coloured algae will grow if the light is too weak, and excessive growth of green algae or the appearance of blue-green algae suggests that the light is too strong. It is then usually sufficient to switch off one lamp.

In the tropics the maximum length of daylight is sixteen hours. This is the period during which the fishes and plants need light. It is no use just switching on the lights during the evening. In fact it is probably best to fit an electric time clock into the circuit so that the lighting comes on at the proper time and the fishes receive the amount of light and darkness they would in the wild. In tropical waters, most of which lie close to the equator, there is no great seasonal difference in the amount of daylight. For many fishes the arrival of dawn (or the switching on of lighting in the aquarium) acts as a signal. Some, for instance, spawn at this time of day. Similarly at twilight many species, such as groupers, look for a suitable place to spend the night, and in those that protect their brood, one can observe the parent fishes gathering the young into a hole or pit, or in the case of mouthbrooding cichlids into the parent's mouth. Fishes, like humans, can adapt themselves to a rhythm of night and day, but they suffer if this is disturbed, just as humans do when they fly in a fast aircraft across the Atlantic, and suffer what we call jet-lag.

Aquarium accessories and spare parts

The aquarist must always ensure that his technical equipment is kept in full working order, otherwise he may suffer loss of money and, more particularly, of valuable fishes. Repairs to equipment often take several weeks, assuming one can find someone to do the work. Fortunately, however, aquarium dealers stock plenty of spare parts for the main items of aquarium equipment.

Tank size length × width × height in cm (inches in brackets)	Capacity in litres (gallons in brackets)	No.	Fluorescent tubes required
60 × 25 × 40 (c. 24 × 10 × 16)	60 (13)	1	20W Gro-lux (in front of tank)
		1	20W Universal white
80 × 26 × 38 (c. 32 × 10 × 15)	79 (17)		as above
80 × 40 × 50 (c. 32 × 16 × 20)	160 (35)	1	20W Gro-lux (in front)
		1	20W Universal white
		1	20W Warm tone de luxe
100 × 30 × 40 (c. 40 × 12 × 16)	120 (26)		as above
100 × 40 × 50 (c. 40 × 16 × 20)	200 (44)	1	20W Gro-lux
		1	25W Universal white
		1	25W Warm tone de luxe
130 × 50 × 50 (c. 52 × 20 × 20)	325 (71½)	1	40W Gro-lux (in front)
		1	20W Warm tone de luxe
		1	40W Universal white

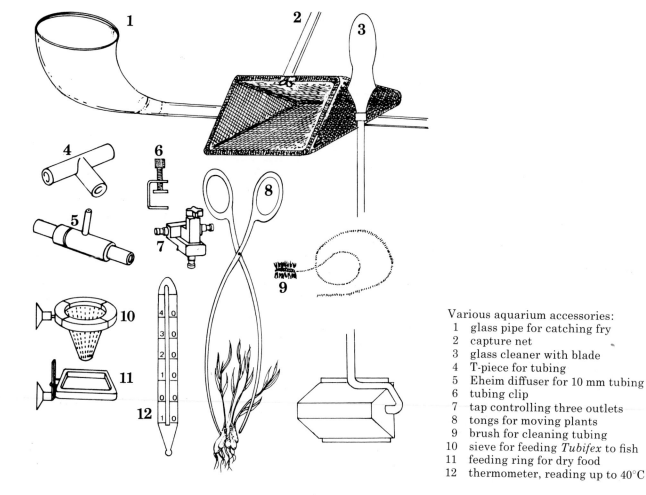

Various aquarium accessories:
1 glass pipe for catching fry
2 capture net
3 glass cleaner with blade
4 T-piece for tubing
5 Eheim diffuser for 10 mm tubing
6 tubing clip
7 tap controlling three outlets
8 tongs for moving plants
9 brush for cleaning tubing
10 sieve for feeding *Tubifex* to fish
11 feeding ring for dry food
12 thermometer, reading up to 40°C

In addition, several miscellaneous items will be needed (see above). These include nets of various sizes for catching fishes and an aquarium scraper for cleaning the glass, since ordinary domestic pot scourers are liable to scratch the glass. A pair of forceps or tongs will be useful for picking up plants, or for moving them around in the tank. A thermometer is essential, so that the temperature of the water can be checked at any time. Plastic taps can be used for adjusting the flow of air from a diaphragm pump, but they occasionally break, and it is really simpler to have a tubing clamp of the type used in chemical laboratories. A long, thin brush is useful for cleaning the plastic tubing connecting the tank and the filter.

Setting up the aquarium

The type of material covering the bottom of an aquarium must be chosen with some care. This material, generally known as the substrate, is of primary importance to some of the plants, but certain fish species will burrow in it.

The most suitable materials are coarse river sand with a particle diameter of 1.5 mm (c. $\frac{1}{16}$ in) and gravel (diameter 3–4 mm, c. $\frac{1}{8}$ in), both of which are sold by aquarium dealers. Finer sand is not suitable as it packs too closely so that the water in it tends to stagnate. Movement of water through the substrate is essential for the maintenance of the bacteria living among the sand grains. These micro-organisms are responsible for the breakdown of various waste products and they are indeed invisible friends of the aquarist. Pale sand and sharp quartz sand are also unsuitable because they reflect the light and this has a disturbing effect on the fishes.

The substrate must be previously washed to get rid of any detritus. It is always possible that sand or gravel, although apparently clean, may contain the eggs of snails or other organisms that might be unwelcome in the aquarium. These can be destroyed by putting the sand or gravel into a large plastic container filled with water to which potassium permanganate is added to give a dark red colour. This should be thoroughly stirred and left to stand for one or two days. The water is then poured off and the sand or gravel washed several times in fresh water.

The question of the correct composition of the substrate always gives rise to argument. Some aquarists mix a lower layer of sand with loam, from which the plant roots can derive certain nutrients. Although the substrate is primarily intended for the plants, in fact very few of them take in the major part of their nutrients through their roots. Most water plants take in their nutrients in dissolved form directly from the water, through the whole of the submerged surface. On the other hand marsh plants, such as *Cryptocoryne*, derive their nutrients mainly through the roots.

For true water plants the substrate serves primarily as a suitable medium for anchorage. To compensate for certain deficiencies the water can from time to time be enriched with special liquid fertilizer, obtainable from aquarium dealers.

Some fishes and plants require extremely soft water, and for these it is essential that the substrate is quite free from any snail or other mollusc shells or parts of them, as these contain calcium, which will soon increase the hardness of the water.

Apart from the substrate, all decorative rocks must be thoroughly scrubbed with a brush and washed under running water. Pieces of igneous rock, such as granite, gneiss, quartz and basalt are ideal for this purpose, but sedimentary rocks such as limestone, marble and sandstone ought not to be used when the water has to be kept soft, as they will increase its hardness. It is quite easy to test whether a rock contains calcium; just put a few drops of hydrochloric or sulphuric acid onto it. If it effervesces the rock contains calcium and should not be used in soft water.

Flat rocks are good for tank decoration as they can be arranged to form caves or holes of various sizes, which provide hiding-places for the fishes. If the tank is to be used for large cichlids, which dig vigorously, the rockwork has to be very firmly constructed to prevent it being undermined and collapsing. If a small amount of cement is used it should be sealed, when thoroughly dry, with an epoxy resin. If this is not done the cement may release toxic substances into the water.

For dwarf cichlids, which are rather more sensitive than their larger relatives, many aquarists use peat blocks. These can be cut relatively easily to provide holes, caves and tunnels, but they need a good soaking to remove the air.

The appearance of a tank can often be greatly improved by installing suitably decorative rockwork fixed in front of the rear glass. A large piece of slate is good for this purpose. It should be glued onto the back wall with silicone rubber. The advantage of using the latter material is that it can later be cut through with a long sharp knife if one wishes to remove the slate. Other decorative rocks can now be put into the tank before the substrate is added. Well-washed tree roots are also useful in a tank. They should not just lie on the substrate but should be raised up above it so that the space beneath them can provide shelter for the fishes. Most fishes, particularly when at rest, try to hide so that they cannot be seen from the water surface. In among the rocks and roots there can be small groups of aquatic plants, some of which can be species that grow up and have broad leaves that float at the surface. If bamboos are used, and they can be very attractive, they must be thoroughly disinfected in hydrogen peroxide, washed, dried and the bottom end sealed with epoxy resin. They can be arranged in irregular groups as they would be in the wild.

After the vegetation has been planted, a layer of rounded basalt chips can be spread over the substrate. This makes it darker. Peat can also be used but this is not done so much nowadays, except when keeping egg-laying toothcarps. In such cases a layer of peat 1–2 cm ($\frac{1}{3}$–$\frac{3}{4}$ in) thick would be appropriate but this will, of course, need to be renewed from time to time.

The appearance of the substrate can also be improved by giving it different levels. It is no good just heaping up piles of sand or gravel, as these will quite rapidly become flattened out. It is more appropriate to build the rocks into a series of terraces, each of which will hold some of the substrate and a few plants.

The use of plastics

Plastics are of course widespread in everyday life, and many different kinds have been used in the aquarium. However, as with all aquarium materials, it is quite essential that any new or unknown plastic should be tested, in order to ensure that it is not releasing toxic substances into the water. Silicone rubber can safely be used as a form of glue, and it sets under the influence of humidity. On the other hand, many household glues require a certain amount of warmth for hardening.

Mention has already been made of epoxy resins which form an excellent hard coating for aquarium purposes, but they must only be applied to absolutely dry objects. Incidentally these resins, when liquid, give off toxic fumes which can be very dangerous, so they should be used only in areas that are properly ventilated.

The water

Natural waters are known to vary considerably in quality and composition, depending largely upon their origin. With the exception of distilled water, which is an artificial product, all waters contain some dissolved matter which they acquire as they pass through different kinds of soils and rocks.

In contrast to sea water, which covers enormous continuous areas and is very uniform in composition, the waters of rivers and lakes are very much influenced by the structure of the surrounding country, e.g. marshland, limestone uplands or estuaries. Sea water contains large amounts of minerals, originally derived from soils and rock, and it is very hard. This is not so in the case of most rivers. The Rio Negro in South America, for instance, has extremely soft water, poor in minerals, for it flows through areas where calcium is almost completely lacking. This dark brown water contains a large amount of humic acids, derived from flooded marshland, leaves and rotting timber, and it has a high content of carbonic acid, giving a very acid pH. This water also has no ammonia, nitrite or nitrate. Fishes coming from such an aquatic environment therefore have special requirements and are often difficult to keep, and particularly to breed, in ordinary urban tap water, much of which is hard. The aquarist must therefore understand the nature of different waters so that he can create a suitable environment for his fishes.

Water hardness

There are two types of hardness, namely carbonate hardness and non-carbonate hardness. The two together make up the total hardness. Various methods of measuring hardness have been devised, but for the aquarist the most convenient is the German system, in which one degree of hardness (1° DH) is the equivalent of 10 milligrams of calcium oxide dissolved in 1 litre of water. British and American degrees of hardness are expressed as parts per million of calcium carbonate, 1 British or US degree being 14.3 parts per million of calcium carbonate. Conversion of these two systems is quite easy:

British or US degrees = $DH \times \frac{56}{100}$
German degrees = British or US degrees $\times \frac{100}{56}$

The hardness of the aquarium water is often of decisive importance when keeping certain fish species. Carbonate or temporary hardness is due to the presence of calcium carbonate, and it can be removed by boiling. Non-carbonate or permanent hardness is due to the presence of various compounds, mainly calcium sulphate and certain salts of magnesium. This type of hardness can be removed only by chemical

Kits for testing water (pH etc.) mostly produce a colour which is then compared with the colours on a standard scale

means (e.g. sodium phosphate, Permutit). The following table is intended as a guide to hardness, distilled water having 0° DH:

Very soft water = 0–4° DH
Soft water = 5–8° DH
Medium-hard water = 0–12° DH
Fairly hard water = 13–18° DH
Hard water = 19–30° DH
Very hard water = over 30° DH

In recent years the hardness of the water used in some towns and cities has fluctuated. This is usually because the demand has become so great that new sources from different areas have had to be tapped. It is therefore advisable to test the hardness of mains water from time to time.

If the mains water is much too hard it can be modified by the addition of distilled water, although this may be quite expensive to do. It is, however, worthwhile doing, particularly if this improves the chance of breeding certain fishes. The amount of distilled water required can be calculated if one knows the hardness of the mains water and the type of water required. If, for example, the mains water is 16° DH and distilled water is 0° DH and the aquarist wants a water with a hardness of 2° DH, then:

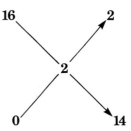

This diagram shows that fourteen parts of distilled water must be mixed with two parts of mains water to give a water with a hardness of 2° DH.

Temporary hardness can, of course, be removed by boiling the water, but it will very slowly return as the water takes up carbon dioxide again, so that bicarbonate is formed.

More rarely, the aquarist may have water that is too soft for his purpose. For example, many of the cichlids from African lakes require hard water. This can be obtained by adding a small amount of a solution of pure calcium sulphate, until the desired hardness is obtained.

The pH value

This is a measure that denotes the acidic or basic (alkaline) nature of a water. The letters pH stand for *pondus Hydrogenii* or the weight of hydrogen. Water consists of H_2O molecules, dissociated into positively charged hydrogen ions (H^+) and negatively charged hydroxyl ions (HO^-). In neutral or distilled water the number of H and HO ions is the same, and the H ions in a litre of water weigh 10^{-7} grams or 0.0000001 grams, while the HO ions weigh the same. This figure is known as the pH value of the water. For sake of convenience one does not write the whole number but only the logarithm of the hydrogen value omitting the negative sign. Thus the pH value of neutral water is 7, written as pH 7. The pH of rain and melted snow is also 7. In acid water the pH value is less than 7, in alkaline it is greater. Waters of the temperate zone mostly have pH values between 7.5 and 9 and are therefore slightly alkaline (moor and marshland waters form an exception). On the other hand, most tropical waters have pH values between 5 and 6.8, and are therefore acid to slightly acid. Naturally, there are exceptions and the best known are the waters of the central African lakes. Although the River Zaire, which is not far away, has slightly acid water (pH 6.5), Lake Tanganyika has water of about pH 8.8 and Lake Malawi about pH 8.0. Further to the north Lake Rudolf, which is poor in fish, has a pH between 9.5 and 10.0. However, even in the soda lakes of East Africa (e.g. Lake Magadi), with a pH of about 11.5 and a specific gravity of 1015 to 1030 (sea water has a specific gravity of about 1025), there are still some fishes (e.g. *Tilapia grahami*), a point which again emphasizes the ability of fishes to adapt.

It is no longer difficult to measure pH, as aquarium dealers supply special kits for this purpose. The pH can be lowered by adding very small amounts of dilute phosphoric acid (3%) to the water, but this procedure is difficult and not to be recommended for the beginner. When the water is already very soft it can be acidified by adding tannins. These may be in the form of oak bark or leaves, willow roots or nutshells, or tannin can be purchased. In the latter case dissolve 0.1–0.3 grams of tannin in 10 litres of water, allow to stand for 4 days and then add to the fish tank. However, most aquarists would prefer to use a peat extract or preferably to filter the tank water through peat. It is often sufficient for the tank to have a back wall made of peat blocks. A peat filter should be renewed every two weeks. Aquarium waters treated with peat are particularly suitable for the maintenance of species of *Nannostomus*, *Aphyosemion*, *Symphysodon* as well as neon tetras and harlequin fishes. If the amount of tannins becomes too high the fishes may not be affected, but the plants soon start to suffer. Preparations of so-called black water should be used with great care, as an overdose will make the aquarium water so dark that one cannot see through it. To test for the correct colour, fill a test-tube to a depth of 10 cm (c. 4 in) with the water concerned and view it from above against a white background. It should have an amber-yellow colour. Any excess tannin can be removed by filtration through peat or reduced by replacement of some of the water.

The effects of hardness and pH on fishes vary considerably. Many labyrinth fishes, rasboras and various species of *Hyphessobrycon* like a pH between 6 and 7, whereas most barbs, some catfishes (e.g. *Otocinclus*) and African cichlids (e.g. *Hemichromis*) only do well when the pH is 7.0–8.5. There are relatively few fishes which require a pH between 5 and 6, and a water hardness of 3–6° DH. These include the characins *Paracheirodon innesi*, *Cheirodon axelrodi*, *Hyphessobrycon heterorhabdus*, *Nannostomus trifasciatus* and *Micralestes interruptus*, the rasboras *Rasbora heteromorpha* and *R. maculatus*, the species of *Aphyosemion* and other egg-laying toothcarps, and the cichlids *Symphysodon discus*, *S. aequifasciata* and some species of *Apistogramma*.

In contrast, there are other fishes, such as the mollies of the genus *Poecilia*, which require slightly brackish water, so in the aquarium they should be kept in water containing 1 heaped tablespoon or 30 grams of sea salt per litre ($1\frac{3}{4}$ pints). The salt should be dissolved in a small quantity of warm water, and added gradually to the tank, with constant stirring.

In the tropics a certain amount of lake and river water evaporates the whole time, but this is replaced by rain. In the aquarium some evaporation will also take place, and this should be replaced by soft water, because the percentage of dissolved salts will increase as water evaporates. It would, therefore, be wrong to add hard water as this would still further increase the salt content. When carrying out a renewal of a proportion of the water, care should be taken to see that any small bubbles introduced are not allowed to settle and remain on fishes and plants.

In the tropical areas from which most aquarium fishes come the water is usually very soft, and poor in dissolved minerals. Some waters in the Amazon basin may, for instance, have a pH value as low as 4.5–4.9. Yet in the wild, fishes such as the cardinal tetra *(Cheirodon axelrodi)* live in this water. Fishes that come from such waters poor in mineral salts (soft waters) need to have the same type of water for breeding, even though as adults they may have been acclimatized in the aquarium to living in a harder, mineral-rich water. The reason for this lies in the structure of the eggs and sperm, which are single cells surrounded by a very thin membrane, and containing water with dissolved salts. The eggs and sperms are also surrounded by water containing dissolved salts. Thus there are two fluids, separated only by a thin semi-permeable membrane, which appear to be similar, but are often not so. If the two fluids contain the same amount of dissolved substance there will be no movement of water from one to another. If, however, the eggs and sperms of fishes that come from soft-water areas are put in water with a greater concentration of dissolved substances, water will pass into the cells faster than it passes out, and the cells will swell and burst. This is a process which many aquarists have observed.

If the local water is too hard it can of course be diluted with distilled water to reduce its hardness, but this would be an expensive process. Some aquarists travel to areas with soft water and bring it back in containers, but this is also expensive, and time-consuming. The best method is to remove the hardness, using water-softening equipment such as is now available on the market. This will remove all the salts and leave a deionized water which is biologically comparable with distilled water, and its pH should be about 7. Filtration through peat will lower the pH. In theory, rain water should also be soft and suitable for the aquarium, but nowadays in many industrial areas the water may be heavily polluted.

Living communities in the aquarium

We have so far been considering the abiotic or non-living factors which affect an aquarium, and we may now turn to the biotic relationships, involving the interaction of the living plants and animals.

From the ecological viewpoint there are three main groups of living organisms: *the producers*, which make organic compounds from inorganic substances, utilizing energy from the sun; *the consumers*, which use these organic substances for growth and maintenance of their bodies and for reproduction; and *the destroyers*, such as bacteria and fungi which once more break down the complicated organic materials into their original inorganic components. An organic cycle is only complete when all three groups are present within a living community. This is what happens in nature, but in the aquarium a true, unbroken natural cycle is scarcely feasible, at any rate over a period of time. Nevertheless, by understanding what happens in the wild, the aquarist can produce a model which is very close to nature. For an aquarium is a miniature world in which green plants (the producers), fishes and other animals (the consumers) and micro-organisms in the substrate (the destroyers) all play an essential role.

Aquarium plants

Plants in a fish tank are often considered primarily in terms of decoration, but this is not the whole story. Aquatic plants and fishes use oxygen for respiration and release carbon dioxide. During the day fishes use oxygen for respiratory purposes and release carbon dioxide, which is used by green plants for assimilation. This is the process in which the plants, possessing the green pigment chlorophyll, take in water and mineral salts, and are able by using the sun's energy to build up organic substances, such as sugars. Animals cannot do this, the ability to do so being restricted to green plants. During assimilation in daylight, the plants release excess oxygen which is used by the fishes for respiration. Thus there is a state of biological equilibrium (see below).

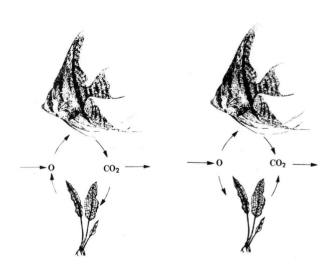

Gaseous exchange between water plants and fishes
left: by day
right: at night

During the night, however, when there is no sunlight, the plants cease to assimilate, but take up some oxygen and release excess carbon dioxide. Their oxygen requirement is, however, so small that the amount they remove does not affect the resting fishes. In general, an aquarium tank has its lowest oxygen content and its highest carbon dioxide content in the morning, at about 0900 hours, but normally this does not constitute a hazard. It is only if the tank has no aeration and contains too many plants and fishes, that the accumulation of carbon dioxide may become serious.

The amount of oxygen released into the water by the plants depends upon the total surface area of the leaves. The larger the area the greater the amount of oxygen produced. In plants with large, flat leaves the total surface area is proportionately less than it is in those with numerous, fine feathery leaflets, such as are found in *Cabomba, Myriophyllum, Elodea* and Java moss *(Vesicularia)*. The planting of a tank should also take account of the light conditions. Plants that require much light and grow rapidly should be put in those parts of the tank that receive most light. Such plants will tend to overshadow smaller ones, but these are often plants which do not need so much light. Delicate, feathery plants almost always need a lot of light, and they do not tolerate algae growing on them.

Aquatic plants fulfill one more important task in the aquarium, for they help to keep the water clean. Unlike land plants, many of those that live in the water are able to take up mineral salts through their general surface as well as through the roots. In this way plants acquire many dissolved substances, which they use in building up their tissues.

Faeces from the fishes and, to a lesser extent, decaying leaves form detritus on the bottom and in a well-established tank this will mostly be broken down by micro-organisms in the substrate into substances that are then taken up by the plants. Excess detritus is almost always a sign that the tank contains too many fishes, so that the biological equilibrium has been upset. Some fish species, of course, burrow in the substrate and eat detritus.

In general, large active fishes have a high oxygen consumption, and at least some of their requirements can be supplied by having plants in greater numbers than one would for smaller species. The arrangement of the plants must also be related to the types of fishes in the tank. Some, such as labyrinth fishes, do well in an aquarium with dense vegetation, but for fishes from open waters that like plenty of space for swimming, planting should be restricted to a dense group in each rear corner, and a few scattered plants along the side and rear walls.

Some fishes use a group of feathery plants as a spawning site. Labyrinth fishes will often make their bubble nests close to floating plants, while others like the half shade produced by such plants. Angelfishes like to bite and tear broad leaves, so their tank should have tough plants such as *Vallisneria*, *Sagittaria* and Amazon sword plants *(Echinodorus)*. Small shoaling fishes with luminescent markings look best in a shady place with a densely planted background and strong overhead lighting; here one could use *Cryptocoryne* species, which prefer subdued light, in the background and have a few Amazon sword plants under the bright light. Cichlids are often difficult to keep together with plants because they dig so vigorously, and here it is best to put the plants in small flowerpots and anchor them firmly in the bottom. Many fishes disturb the surface of the substrate, stirring up mud, which settles on the plants. This coating of mud is particularly undesirable in the case of plants with feathery leaves, and indeed plants of this type should not be used in tanks with cichlids, harlequin fishes and some other fishes which regard them as delicacies.

It might be thought better to plant a tank with species from the same region as the fishes, but this is not absolutely necessary. Most aquarium plants like water that is soft, slightly acid and warm. Species of *Cryptocoryne* should be planted in water with a maximum depth of 30 cm (12 in), for they are originally marsh plants. If they do not appear to be doing well they probably need a somewhat softer water.

Aquarium plants should not be positioned at random. The individual species should be gathered in small groups, separated from one another by rockwork or roots. Furthermore, the individual plants in each group should not be planted too close together, as they will soon grow and spread. Two or three species would be sufficient for a small tank, possibly one or two more for a large aquarium.

If the tank has terraced rockwork, the marsh plants can be planted at the higher level so that they can soon grow up above the surface and possibly flower. Small plants can be put towards the front, but not in such numbers as to obscure the rest of the tank.

At least once a year the tank should be treated as one would a small-scale garden. Plants that have grown too large and bushy can be removed, thus giving more light and space for the others. Naturally, all withered plants and damaged leaves must be removed. A careful check on the accumulation of detritus should be made at more frequent intervals. A small amount of detritus will do no harm and may actually provide some nutrient for the plants, but large accumulations will only consume a great amount of oxygen.

Certain plants do not do well together, usually because the more robust ones crowd out those that grow more slowly. As an example, it is not a good idea to plant *Cryptocoryne* species close to *Vallisneria* or *Sagittaria*. Finally, condensation water dripping down from the tank cover will damage floating plants.

Before planting can begin the tank must be thoroughly cleaned to remove all traces of filamentous algae, snail spawn and pockets of dirt, and should then be disinfected for about twenty minutes with a solution of potassium permanganate (enough to give a deep pink colour). An additional bath in hydrogen peroxide (1 teaspoonful to each litre (1¾ pints) of water) for five to ten minutes is also recommended. The tank must then be washed out with fresh water. The plants should now be carefully rinsed and their roots slightly pruned, as this promotes growth, and the tank filled with water to a depth of 10 cm (3¾ in).

The tallest plants should be put in at the back, close to the rear wall, while smaller species are planted in part of the foreground. Care should always be taken to ensure that the roots are arranged as they would be in nature. Thus *Cryptocoryne* and *Vallisneria* have roots that descend vertically, so a hole should be made in the substrate and the root inserted carefully and spread out as much as the hole will allow. The roots are then carefully covered with substrate,

gently firmed with the fingers, and the whole plant pulled upwards very gently, so that the top of the roots is just clear of the substrate. Each plant requires an area of about 5 sq cm (2 sq in), but the exact space will depend upon its rate of growth and final size. Plants that grow large, such as *Cryptocoryne griffithii, C. ciliata* or *C. beckettii* should be planted at least 15 cm (6 in) apart.

Aquatic plants that take in water and mineral through their general surface can be inserted in the substrate as rootless cuttings, after removal of the lower two or three leaves. Flat stones can be used to anchor these cuttings until they have rooted. It is a good idea to insert four to six cuttings in a group, each 1–2 cm (c. ½ in) apart. Plants such as *Kalmus*, with horizontal creeping rootstocks, should be put in at an angle.

Aquatic plants that derive their nutrients from the substrate by means of their roots include *Aponogeton, Echinodorus* and *Cryptocoryne*. These can be planted in shallow flowerpots in a mixture of two-thirds loam and aquarium peat to one-third of the substrate being used in the rest of the tank. This method is also useful for tanks containing cichlids that dig extensively, and it has the advantage that the plants can be removed without damage to their roots when the tank substrate is being cleaned. The best time for planting is spring, when young plants have finished their resting period (November to January) and are beginning to grow rapidly.

Propagation of aquarium plants is mostly done by vegetative means, that is, by cuttings, runners and division of plants or roots. Runners should not be separated from the parent plant until they have formed a sufficient number of roots. Cuttings are obtained by taking branches or by pruning back a main stem. Division of plants should be done in the spring. Certain plants form winter buds and these should be collected in autumn and kept over winter in a shallow dish with sand and some water in a cool, frostproof place. About the middle of February they can be brought into the aquarium room, and gradually brought up to the temperature of the tank water. They can then be put into a suitable tank where, in the warm water and bright light, they will soon start to grow again.

It is possible to divide aquatic plants into seven

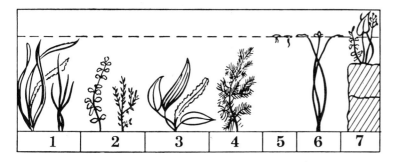

Water-plant types:
1 with strap-like leaves
2 with coarse or mossy leaves
3 with long stalks
4 with feathery leaves
5 floating plants
6 rooted plants with floating leaves
7 marsh plants

groups on the basis of their form and particularly of their leaf structure. These are 1: plants with strap-like leaves; 2: plants with coarse or mossy leaves; 3: plants with long stalks; 4: plants with feathery leaves; 5: floating plants; 6: rooted plants with floating leaves, and 7: marsh plants.
Group 1: these are good oxygen producers, which need plenty of light. Runners can be held down on the bottom by small stones. Most of these plants take in nutrients by the roots, so they can be planted in small pots.
Group 2: good oxygen producers, which also serve as spawning sites and provide shelter. They should be planted in small groups in a well-lit position. These plants take in their nutrients through their general surface, not by the roots. Propagation is by runners or cuttings.
Group 3: these require soft water and subdued light. Some species can be grown in pots. *Cryptocoryne* species should not be planted close to *Vallisneria* or *Sagittaria*.
Group 4: good oxygen producers. Some, such as *Cabomba*, require soft water and good light. These plants provide shelter and spawning sites, and can be planted in groups. The roots are only used for anchorage. Propagation by cuttings.
Group 5: good spawning plants which require bright light and plenty of air, so the tank should not have a cover. This will also prevent condensation water from falling on them. Only about one-third of the surface should be covered with floating plants.
Group 6: require plenty of light from above and are best grown in small pots.
Group 7: suitable for a tank where they can send shoots up above the water surface.
  The following notes on aquarium plants should help the aquarist to choose suitable species, bearing in mind the type of water in the tank and the fish species which are to live in it. The group is indicated by the figure immediately following the scientific name.

Acorus gramineus (1)
A grass-like plant with leaves up to 40 cm (16 in) long, which is also good for a marsh aquarium. It does not like high temperatures over a long period, but thrives in temperate water.

Acorus gramineus

Anubias nana

Aponogeton madagascariensis

Anubias nana (3)
A marsh plant of the African tropical rain-forests, which likes soft water at a temperature around 24°C (75°F) and good but not bright light. It does not do so well when the leaves are continuously submerged.

Aponogeton madagascariensis (formerly *A. fenestralis*) (3)
A very decorative plant, known as the Madagascar lace-plant which is, unfortunately, not very easy to grow. It produces winter buds which require a resting period at a reduced temperature. These buds will die if kept at a high temperature.

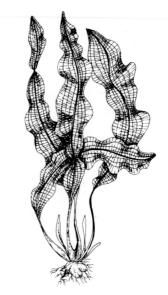

Aponogeton ulvaceus

Aponogeton ulvaceus (3)
This is another decorative plant from Madagascar, with pale yellow-green wavy leaves. It grows quite large so it should be given an uncrowded position on its own in a large tank. In general, it is not difficult to grow. Other species in the genus include *A. bernierianus*, *A. crispus*, *A. elongatus*, *A. natans* and *A. undulatus*.

Bacopa monniera (2)

This is originally a marsh plant, but it does extremely well in an aquarium tank. It comes from tropical and subtropical regions and prefers a coarse sandy substrate, soft to medium-hard water and good light. Propagation is by cuttings. Owing to its wide distribution it can tolerate a wide range of temperatures (15–26°C or 59–79°F). The large-leaved related species *B. amplexicaulis* is not so suitable for growing continually submerged.

Barclaya longifolia

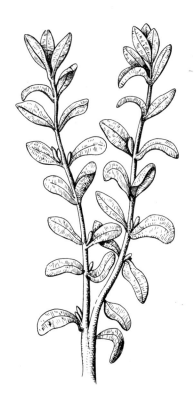

Bacopa monniera

Cabomba aquatica (4)

The species of *Cabomba* have a wide distribution extending from southern North America to Central and South America. For aquarium purposes the best species is *C. aquatica*, but it is not always grown correctly. It requires very soft water and plenty of light. Propagation is by cuttings which can be inserted in flowerpots containing a mixture of loam and coarse sand, which are then placed in the aquarium tank. The water temperature should be 20–28°C (68–82°F). Other species in the genus include *C. australis*, *C. caroliniana* and *C. piauhyensis*.

Barclaya longifolia (3)

This is a handsome plant from the tropical rain-forests of south-east Asia. It has certain special requirements and is really only suitable for the expert. It can be planted in a tank with a substrate of loam and coarse sand, with very soft water at a temperature of 25–28°C (77–82°F). Care should be taken to ensure that the substrate does not become too cold. This plant should not be grown in a tank with a population of snails.

Cabomba aquatica

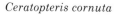
Ceratopteris cornuta

Ceratopteris thalictroides, broad-leaved form

Ceratopteris cornuta (5)

This is a floating water fern admirably adapted for the aquarium, provided there is sufficient space between the surface of the water and the tank cover. It thrives even better if the tank is left uncovered. The water should be soft to medium-hard, at a temperature of 20–30°C (68–86°F). If well cared for and given sufficient surface area a single plant can attain a diameter of about 50 cm (20 in). Propagation is by daughter plantlets which are produced vegetatively.

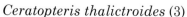
Ceratopteris thalictroides, fine-leaved form

Ceratopteris thalictroides (3)

This plant, sometimes known as Sumatra fern, occurs in more than one form. Some specimens have finely divided leaves, others have broader leaves, but they all belong to the same species. They should not be planted too deep in the substrate. Propagation is by daughter plantlets.

Cryptocoryne affinis (formerly *C. haerteliana*) (3)

The genus *Cryptocoryne* has a large number of species and many of these are very widely grown as aquarium plants. From time to time new species appear on the market. *C. affinis* comes from Malaya and grows to a height of 15 cm (6 in). The uppersides of the leaves are dark blue-green, the undersides pale green (when kept in subdued light) or wine-red (in bright light). These plants can be grown in shallow flowerpots with a mixture of loam and peat covered with coarse sand. They require a moderate amount of light, soft water and a temperature of 22–26°C

(72–79°F). The species of *Cryptocoryne* should be planted in groups and left to grow undisturbed; in fact frequent re-planting is not recommended, and they will not tolerate a cold substrate.

Cryptocoryne affinis

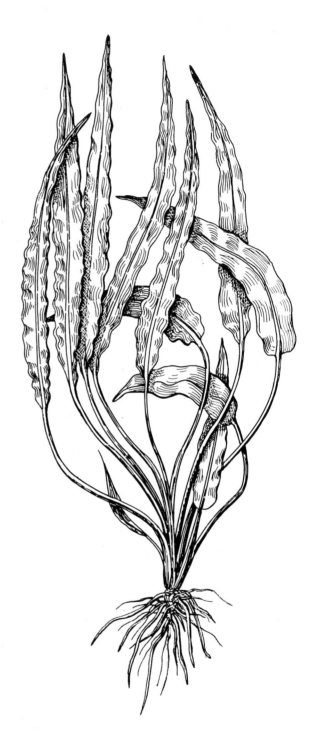

Cryptocoryne balansae

Cryptocoryne balansae
(formerly *C. somphongsii*) (3)
This is one of the larger species of *Cryptocoryne*, sometimes reaching a height of about 30 cm

(12 in). It comes from Vietnam and Thailand. The wavy leaves are pale green on both sides. In general this species can be grown in the same way as *C. affinis*, but it can also be planted on its own, not in a group.

Cryptocoryne ciliata

Cryptocoryne nevillii

Cryptocoryne ciliata (3)
A widely distributed plant in south-east Asia, this species has bright green leaves and reaches a height of 40 cm (16 in) and will in fact grow up above the water surface if not prevented by the tank cover. It requires bright lighting but otherwise should be grown like *C. affinis*.

Cryptocoryne nevillii (3)
A smaller species, originally from Ceylon (Sri Lanka), and very suitable for planting in the foreground of an aquarium tank, where it should spread quite quickly.

Cryptocoryne purpurea (3)
A small, very decorative species, scarcely reaching a height of 10 cm ($3\frac{3}{4}$ in), which comes from Malaya. The leaves are dark green on both sides, the undersides having a reddish tinge. They become darker as they grow older. To be kept like *C. affinis*.

Cryptocoryne purpurea

Cryptocoryne wendtii (3)
This is a species from south-east Asia which has not been known for very long as an aquarium plant. It reaches a height of 12 cm ($4\frac{3}{4}$ in) and usually grows rapidly. The uppersides of the leaves are dark, the undersides pale green with a reddish tinge. In general, this plant can be cultivated in the same way as *C. affinis*. Other species suitable for the aquarium are *C. beckettii*, *C. blassii*, *C. griffithii*, *C. longicauda*, *C. johorensis*, *C. versteegii* (from Papua–New Guinea and only 6 cm ($2\frac{1}{4}$ in) in height) and the very tall *C. retrospiralis*.

Echinodorus amazonicus
(formerly *E. brevipedicellatus*) (3)
Species of the genus *Echinodorus* are mostly extremely handsome and are generally known as Amazon sword plants. Their leaves are tough and hard and very few fishes will try to eat them. They grow rapidly and should occasionally be given a fertilizer tablet. *E. amazonicus* is widely distributed in Brazil. It reaches a height of at least 30 cm (12 in) and is very suitable for growing as a specimen plant on its own, possibly in a shallow pot with a mixture of loam and coarse sand. The water should be soft to medium-hard. Propagation is by runners or plantlets that develop vegetatively on the stems.

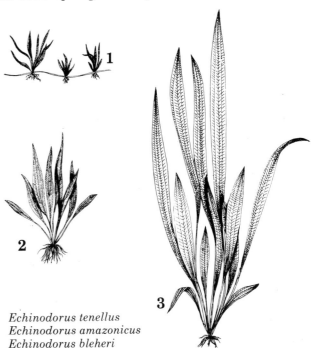

Cryptocoryne wendtii

1   *Echinodorus tenellus*
2   *Echinodorus amazonicus*
3   *Echinodorus bleheri*

Echinodorus bleheri
(formerly *E. paniculatus*) (3)
This is one of the larger members of the genus, reaching a height of at least 40 cm (16 in) and is not at all difficult to grow, in the same way as *E. amazonicus*. Dealers sometimes offer forms with very broad leaves.

Echinodorus cordifolius (3)
This species, originally from Central and South America, is sometimes sold as *E. radicans*. It has heart-shaped leaves on long stems, and grows to a height of about 20 cm ($7\frac{3}{4}$ in). It requires soft water and plenty of light, but the temperature should not be too high.

Echinodorus latifolius
(formerly *E. magdalenensis*) (3)
A small species from Colombia, growing to a height of 15 cm (6 in) at the most. This is an excellent aquarium plant that grows rapidly and should be kept like the other species of *Echinodorus*, except that the water temperature can be much lower (up to about 16°C or 61°F).

Echinodorus latifolius

Echinodorus cordifolius

Echinodorus tenellus (3)
This is a charming small sword plant, 8 cm (3 in) tall at the most, which is particularly suitable for the foreground of a tank. It is sometimes erroneously sold as *Sagittaria microfolia*. It comes originally from tropical and subtropical areas of America. It should be planted in a mixture of sand and gravel, but it is not always easy to keep. Propagation is by runners.

Other species suitable for the aquarium include *E. berteroi*, *E. martii*, *E. muricatus* and *E. nymphaeifolius*.

Eleocharis acicularis (3)
A small North American sedge which looks best when grown in the foreground of a tank. It can be planted in sand alone, and the needle-shaped leaves often reach a height of 20 cm ($7\frac{3}{4}$ in), but usually remain shorter. The water should be soft to medium-hard, at a temperature not exceeding 22°C (72°F). Propagation is by runners. The related *E. vivipara* is also grown.

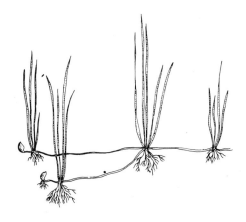

Eleocharis acicularis

Elodea densa (2)
This is a good aquarium plant for beginner aquarists, being robust and fast-growing. It can adapt to a wide range of temperatures, in fact anything between 12° and 28°C (54–82°F), and will grow in subdued or bright light. The water can be medium-hard, and the cuttings can simply be inserted in the sand. The related species *E. canadensis* (Canadian waterweed) and *E. callitrichoides* (Chilean waterweed) are not suitable for tropical tanks as they do not tolerate temperatures above 18°C (64°F). *E. canadensis* is, however, a good plant for a cold-water tank.

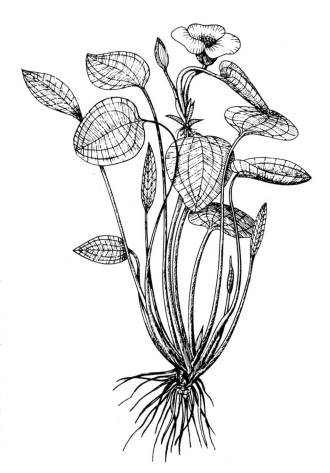

Hydrocleis nymphoides

Elodea densa

Hydrocleis nymphoides (1)
This is a very handsome American plant, but one which is not really suitable for the standard aquarium. It requires a tank with a large surface area and a well-lit, airy position and it does not like condensation water dripping on it. As the stalks of the floating leaves are up to 25 cm (10 in) in length the tank must also be tall enough. This plant can be grown in a flowerpot with a mixture of rich loam and sand in water at a temperature of 22–28°C (72–82°F).

Hygrophyla difformis

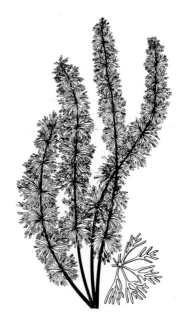

Limnophila indica

Limnobium stoloniferum

Hygrophyla difformis
(formerly *Synnema triflorum*) (4)
This plant from south-east Asia has been used in increasing numbers for aquarium tanks during recent years. It has a certain resemblance to *Ceratopteris* but its leaves are larger and more compact. The individual leaves reach a length of over 10 cm ($3\frac{3}{4}$ in), and under favourable conditions the whole plant grows to a height of about 50 cm (20 in). It requires bright light and soft water at a temperature of 22–28°C (72–82°F), but is quite content if planted in a substrate of pure sand. Propagation is generally by cuttings.

Limnobium stoloniferum (5)
A small South American floating plant to be grown under bright light in very soft water at a temperature of 22–28°C (72–82°F). Under these conditions it lives a long time and propagates itself by runners. The floating leaves have a maximum length of 2 cm ($\frac{3}{4}$ in) and the whole plant is only about 4 cm ($1\frac{1}{2}$ in) across.

Limnophila (Ambulia) indica (4)
This is another aquatic plant with fine feathery leaves, which comes from tropical and subtropical parts of Asia, Australia and Africa. Like *Cabomba* it requires soft water and very

Lobelia cardinalis

Ludwigia natans

bright light. It is propagated by cuttings inserted in little bundles into a mixture of sand and loam. Cut shoots give off a poisonous substance and so the plant must be removed from the tank before being cut or divided. *L. sessiliflora* is also grown as an aquarium plant.

Lobelia cardinalis (2)
A North American plant which should be grown under bright light in water that is not too soft and not too warm (maximum 24°C or 75°F). The substrate should contain some loam. Propagation is by cutting.

Ludwigia natans (2)
A plant from subtropical America which likes a bright light and a temperature not exceeding 25°C (77°F); the water should not be too soft. The leaves are brownish-green above, reddish-violet below. Propagation is by cuttings. This plant appears to have become less popular in recent years, possibly because it does not tolerate the high temperatures of some tropical tanks.

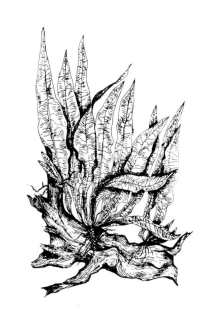

Microsorium pteropus

Microsorium pteropus (1)
Known sometimes as Java fern, this is an undemanding plant which does not root firmly in the substrate but anchors itself loosely in the gravel by its rhizome. It is also very decorative

when grown in narrow cracks in pieces of rock or root. It can reach a height of 30 cm (11¾ in) but is usually smaller. It thrives best at a temperature of 20–28°C (68–82°F) with moderate light, but should not be grown in water that is too soft. Propagation is by daughter plantlets.

Nomaphila stricta

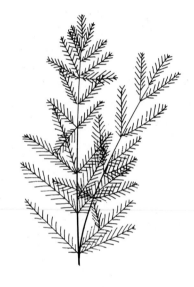

Myriophyllum brasiliense

Nomaphila stricta (1)
An attractive plant from Indonesia and south-east Asia which requires bright light and a warm temperature (22–30°C, 72–86°F), but the water should not be soft. It normally grows quite rapidly. The cuttings should be inserted in groups, and the substrate should not be enriched with nutrients. This plant is rather prone to be attacked by snails.

Myriophyllum brasiliense (4)
This is one of the plants with feathery leaves that require bright light, but not too high a temperature as it comes from subtropical rather than tropical areas (maximum 25°C or 77°F). Nor does it thrive in water that is too soft, and is not suitable for small, shallow tanks. Propagation is by cuttings. Related species, known colloquially as milfoils, also suitable for the aquarium include *M. heterophyllum*, *M. hippuroides* and *M. scabratum*.

Najas kingii (4)
A tropical plant from south-east Asia which can be grown in small groups, taking great care when cuttings are being planted as the stems are very brittle. It requires bright light and soft water, but not at too high a temperature.

Najas kingii

Nymphaea daubenyana (6)

This is one of the water-lilies, a group represented in temperate as well as tropical waters. They are mostly too large for the average tank and they require a large amount of light. However, the plant shown here, which is actually a hybrid, is rather smaller, with oval floating leaves which sometimes reach a length of 20 cm (7¾ in). It should be planted in a flowerpot containing equal parts of humus, loam and coarse sand, not mixed but put into the pot in that order, starting with the humus at the bottom. The water, which must be about 30 cm (12 in) deep, should be as soft as possible and kept at a temperature of 20–30°C (68–86°F). Such plants die back in winter and should then be given a period of rest at about 12°C (54°F).

Nymphaea daubenyana

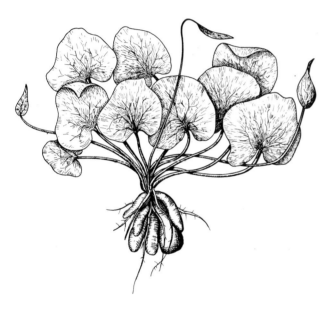

Nymphoides aquatica

Pistia stratiotes (5)

This very beautiful plant does not grow too large for the average tank. It can be kept in quite shallow water, but without a tank cover. It requires bright light and soft water at a temperature of 20–30°C (68–86°F). The roots hang down in the water in bunches, providing shelter for fishes. The leaves can reach a length of 5–15 cm (2–6 in) so this is a plant for a relatively large tank.

Nymphoides aquatica (5)

Sometimes known as the underwater banana plant, from the shape of the roots. This plant comes from eastern North America where it lives in areas of shallow water at fairly low temperatures (not exceeding 15–22°C or 59–72°F). It can be grown in a tank under bright light in soft, slightly acid water, and will often live floating freely. In the aquarium, however, it is probably better to plant the tips of the roots in order to keep it anchored in one place.

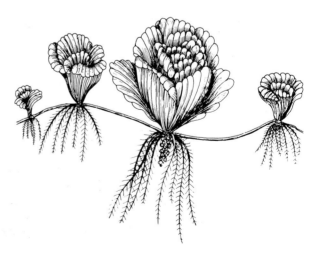

Pistia stratiotes

Riccia fluitans

Sagittaria subulata

Riccia fluitans (5)

This is a very undemanding small plant which is often introduced into aquarium tanks attached to other aquatic plants. It lives entirely at the surface, growing so rapidly that a thick cushion has to be removed every week if the submerged plants are to receive sufficient light. It thrives in soft to medium-hard water and as it needs so much light can be placed immediately below the lamps. Propagation is by division.

Sagittaria subulata (1)

This species, from the subtropical parts of the eastern United States, occurs in two forms. The form *natans* has leaves about 40 cm (16 in) long, whereas in the form *pusilla* the leaves only reach a length of 10 cm ($3\frac{3}{4}$ in). Both forms should be grown under moderate light in a mixture of loam and sand, at a temperature of 25°C (77°F). Under such conditions the plants should produce oval or spoon-shaped floating leaves on long stalks.

Sagittaria platyphylla

Sagittaria platyphylla (1)

Plants of the genus *Sagittaria* are widely used in the aquarium. They come from temperate and subtropical regions and so are correspondingly hardy. *S. platyphylla*, from south-eastern North America, grows to a height of 30 cm (c. 12 in), and so is suitable for planting at the back of a tank. It does best in medium-hard water, but does not require bright light.

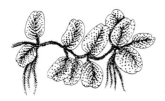

Salvinia auriculata

should be grown under bright light in a sandy substrate, preferably with a little loam, in medium-hard water at a temperature of 12–30°C (54–86°F). This species has a variant form known as *tortifolia* in which the leaves are more closely twisted. There is also another larger species, *V. gigantea*, in which the leaves may grow to a length of 1–2 m (c. 3–6 ft).

Salvinia auriculata (5)

This is a rootless, floating fern from tropical America. The leaves are not more than 1.5 cm (c. $\frac{1}{2}$ in) long, so this is a suitable plant for a small tank. It requires plenty of light and soft to medium-hard water at a temperature of 20–28°C (68–82°F). It does not tolerate condensation water dripping from a tank cover just above it. In fact this attractive little plant is best grown in an uncovered tank.

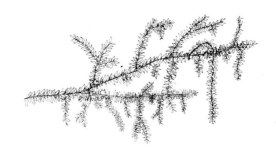

Vesicularia dubyana

Vallisneria spiralis

Vallisneria tortifolia

Vesicularia dubyana (2)

This is a moss often known as Java moss, widely distributed throughout the whole of south-east Asia, Indonesia and the Philippines. The leaves are tiny, normally only 1 mm (c. $\frac{1}{25}$ in) long. The plant can be anchored by a rock, and it provides a good substrate for spawning. Java moss can be grown in almost any kind of water under normal tropical conditions. It does not grow too rapidly, and so requires very little attention.

Vallisneria spiralis (1)

This must be one of the most commonly grown aquarium plants, and indeed it is often the first inmate of a newly established tank. It grows to a height of 60 cm (24 in), and is sometimes confused with *Sagittaria subulata*. *Vallisneria*

The fishes

The average tropical aquarium tank is often set up with an unsuitable mixture of fishes. In many cases the fishes are bought more or less at random, perhaps according to personal taste. This may be all right, but often some of the fishes die quite soon, and one wonders why, for there are no external signs of disease. In such cases the fault may possibly lie in the composition of the fish population. Perhaps one has bought only a single individual of a species that should be kept as a shoal, or young predatory fishes have been introduced which, as they grow, become increasingly aggressive towards the other inmates of the tank. This can occur with many cichlid species which show innate territorial behaviour. As they grow this drive increases and they start to chase other fishes away from what they regard as their own territory. In the confined space of a tank the territorial activities of such cichlids may well lead to the death of other fishes.

To avoid such mistakes it is quite essential that the aquarist should read all he can about the species concerned. The appropriate literature will almost always tell him whether a certain species can be introduced into a community tank, or whether it must be kept in what is known as a species tank, i.e. in a tank on its own.

One of the more interesting ways of setting up a tank is to design a biotope or habitat aquarium. Such a tank would contain only plants and fishes from a given region. For instance, a loach tank would be based on a section of stream in south-east Asia where so many of the loaches live. There could be flat rocks interspersed with coarse and fine gravel and a few roots. Groups of *Cryptocoryne* species could be planted round the edges of the tank, which would contain water kept clear and in motion by a powerful filter. In addition to the loaches (all of which should be species that do not grow too large) there could be a shoal of small barbs, as these would occupy the upper and middle water layers while the loaches lived on the bottom. In setting up this or any other kind of tropical freshwater tank it is always advisable to put the plants in first, and to allow them some time to become established before the fishes are introduced.

The beginner aquarist should start with a few hardy species, such as guppies, platies and swordtails, and should learn to observe these and to improve his methods before going on to what the aquarist regards as the more difficult fishes. Many beginners make the mistake of meddling too frequently with the tank and with the fishes. A newly established tank, in particular, must be given sufficient time to settle down, and this is a matter of weeks rather than days.

A shoal of Sumatra barbs *(Barbus tetrazona)*

Snails

Snails in an aquarium fulfill a special and not unimportant role. In former times, when aquarists were concerned mainly with cold-water fishes, it was recognized that snails act as scavengers, eating up scraps of excess food and also dead fishes, thus reducing the chances of the water becoming fouled.

For a cold-water tank there are several suitable snails which are commonly found in temperate regions. These include the great ramshorn snail *(Planorbis corneus)*, which can also live in warm water, the species *Bulimus tentaculus* up to 10–12 mm (c. $\frac{1}{3}$ in) across, and the much larger river snail *(Viviparus viviparus)*, up to 35 mm (c. $1\frac{1}{4}$ in). All such animals must be kept in a separate tank for a period of about six weeks, as they may carry infectious diseases which can be passed to the fishes.

The ramshorn snail *Planorbis corneus* is commonly seen in tropical freshwater tanks. As a matter of fact it often finds its way into the tank in the form of eggs attached to plants. There is no harm in this as long as the snails do not become too numerous. If their rate of multiplication increases too much they must be culled by hand. The smaller individuals can be squashed against the tank glass, and the fishes will do the rest.

The Malayan pond snail *(Melanoides tuberculata)* is a nocturnal mollusc which makes quite an attractive addition to a tank. During the day these snails move through the substrate, and in doing so they may, of course, do some damage to the plants. They grow to a length of about 2.5 cm (1 in) and produce live young. They do not survive in water that is too soft as they require calcium for the shell, but from 4–6 DH upwards they are quite happy and will breed freely. They thrive at a temperature of about 25°C (77°F).

The various species of *Ampullaria* are perhaps too large for the average aquarium tank, but they are interesting animals to keep, perhaps in a tank on their own. In any case they require quite a lot of space. They are not difficult to feed, as they will eat the same things as the fishes, including *Tubifex*, and they have an enormous appetite for lettuce and algae. It is well worthwhile anchoring a carefully washed lettuce leaf and watching an *Ampullaria* slowly devour it.

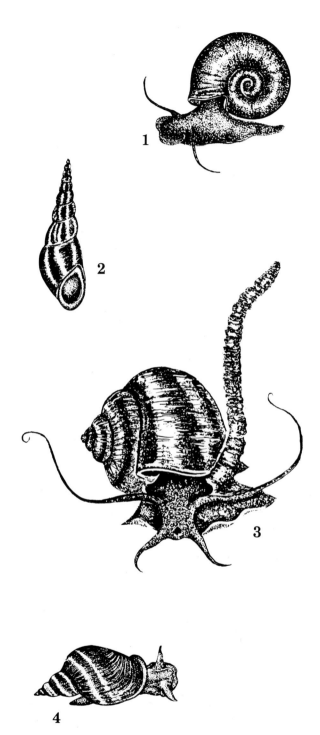

Four snails commonly seen in the aquarium:
1 Ramshorn snail
2 Malayan pond snail
3 *Ampullaria* with proboscis extended
4 *Limnaea*, an unsuitable snail for the aquarium

These snails have a proboscis which can be extended to take in atmospheric air at the surface, and they do this when the water is deficient in oxygen. When not in use the proboscis is withdrawn and cannot be seen. If disturbed the whole snail withdraws into the shell and closes the opening with a kind of lid, known as the operculum. The *Ampullaria* snails, which come originally from South America, will also breed in the aquarium. The eggs are laid on the tank glass above the water line, and they hatch into tiny versions of the adults.

Pond snails of the genus *Limnaea* are not recommended as they are mainly vegetarian and will soon destroy the plants used to decorate the aquarium. They are usually brought in, as eggs, with live food taken from local ponds, and once they have established themselves in a tank they are extremely difficult to eradicate.

In fact most aquarium snails tend to multiply too rapidly, and various methods have been tried for controlling them. The use of chemicals is rather drastic as these will usually kill all the snails. A better method is to introduce one or two pufferfishes, just for a short period. The species *Tetraodon palembangensis* and *T. fluviatilis* are commonly available, and they are very suitable for this purpose. Any *Ampullaria* snails that one wants to keep should be removed from the tanks before the pufferfishes are introduced. The pufferfishes need not be left long in the tank, for they tend to nip the long fins of other species. In spite of their clumsy appearance pufferfishes can actually swim quite rapidly, and it is often difficult to catch them. This is best attempted late in the evening or early in the morning when the fishes are drowsy and easier to handle.

Care of the fish

Feeding

Aquarium plants take their nutrients from the water and the substrate, sometimes supplemented by one of the numerous fertilizer preparations. Fishes, on the other hand, cannot take nutrient in dissolved form from the water. They have to be fed, and here the usual mistakes made by the beginner aquarist are to overfeed, and to supply a diet that is too uniform.

In principle, the fishes should only be given as much food as they will consume in a few minutes. Even in the wild, fishes experience periods when food is scarce, and they do not suffer if they find no food for a period of perhaps one or two days. This would apply, of course, to adult fishes that have been well fed, not to young, growing fishes.

Some aquarists worry about what will happen when they go on holiday, but this is not such a problem as it seems. Provided they have been well fed in the preceding period there is no harm in leaving the fishes unfed for a couple of weeks. It would be wrong, of course, to introduce new fishes to the tank just before going on holiday, as they might bring in disease when there is nobody around to spot it. In addition, there would need to be a time switch for the lighting so that the regular rhythm of night and day is maintained.

In all aquarium tanks small algae will be growing the whole time on the plants and the glass, and they are often overlooked. When food is scarce many fishes discover this vegetarian food, which is nutritious but not fattening.

If an automatic food dispenser is available it is best to use freeze-dried food. This type of food contains all the necessary nutrients and is therefore very suitable for the fishes. For some automatic dispensers it may be found that freeze-dried food is too light and will not drop down out of the container. Fishes that know this kind of food will pick the particles from the surface of the water.

In almost every aquarium tank there is a hierarchy or pecking order within a species or family group, or indeed within the community as a whole, and this is particularly noticeable at feeding time. Sometimes it looks as though all the fishes are going to feed together. Then suddenly one fish, usually a large one, draws apart and starts to make its presence known. This 'boss' fish must feed first and the others must be made aware of this. It is not always possible to be sure about how much food young fishes are getting, so they should be watched under a lens in order to find out the kinds of food they prefer. Their diet can then be suitably adjusted.

It is also important to provide the fishes with plenty of variety. Nowadays, since the advent of freeze-dried foods, the selection has become so wide that there is absolutely no need to restrict the diet to one or two types of food. The diet must, in the first instance, be based on the requirements of the fishes. Thus, active predatory fishes require different food from peaceful species, and in larger quantities. It is pointless to offer a predatory fish, known to require live food, just a few pinches of dried food. Nor will it be attracted by a water-flea. In fact, the smaller the live food, the less likely it will be to attract a predator. In an aquarium teeming with water-fleas it is not uncommon to see a predatory fish retreat into the furthest corner and assume a dark coloration – an unmistakable piscine protest.

The size of the food must relate to the mouth sizes of the different fishes, although even species with a small mouth will sometimes try to swallow relatively large food. For instance, a 3-inch Congo tetra has been observed feeding on mealworms, which have a hard, chitinous armour. The fish would seize a mealworm and chew it backwards and forwards in its mouth until it finally managed to swallow it. Sometimes, as the worm was pushed forwards and protruded from its mouth, another fish would appear and seize the worm, so that a tug-of-war ensued.

The term 'live food' is used in aquarium circles for a wide variety of living animals which can be caught in ponds or out in the field, or bought in aquarist shops. The larger sizes of live food suitable for cichlids and large characins would include young fishes, tadpoles, smooth caterpillars, aquatic insects and their larvae, wood-lice, earthworms, mealworms, snails, bluebottles and other large flying insects. Medium-sized live food would include mosquito larvae, *Tubifex* worms, whiteworms, small or chopped earthworms, water-fleas, small flies and maggots, and aphids. Small live food includes water-fleas and *Cyclops*, small gnat larvae, Grindal worms and microworms, and the nauplii (young stages) of the brine shrimp *Artemia salina*, as well as the larger types of live food chopped up very finely.

If live food is not available one can use grated meat or chopped mussel flesh. Even fishes such as the various discus fishes, regarded as difficult to feed, will eat grated meat if it is properly prepared. In most cases this is made from beef hearts which must be carefully cleaned, leaving only the non-fatty dark red flesh. This can then be chopped up into small cubes and deep-frozen, which renders it easier to grate than raw, unfrozen flesh. The only disadvantage of this type of food is that very fine pieces fall down between the gravel to provide a bonus for the snails.

Dried food includes not only the various brands sold in small containers but also oatflakes, egg yolk and dried yeast. Many fishes require a supplement of plant food, such as washed lettuce leaves, boiled spinach or soaked oatflakes. Very fine food for fish fry is only used in the first few days after hatching. It consists of infusorians (particularly the ciliate protozoans known as slipper animalcules or *Paramecium*), rotifers, small algae and powdered foods. The latter can be bought ready made or it can be prepared by grinding dried food. Chopped foods of all kinds can be made into a kind of gruel which is then pressed through coarse cloth to prevent excess fouling of the tank.

Young fishes are also fond of the larvae or nauplii of *Artemia*. In the wild these small crustaceans live in waters which have a high content of mineral salts, and they feed mainly on plant plankton. *Artemia* eggs are widely available on the market. When placed in water containing a level teaspoonful of cooking salt (25–30 grams) in 1 litre, or about 1 ounce in $1\frac{3}{4}$ pints of water, and kept at a temperature of 22–24°C (72–75°F) they will hatch into nauplii (singular: nauplius) in 24–36 hours. The water should be strongly aerated to keep the eggs moving.

The freshly hatched *Artemia* nauplii must then be removed from the hatching tank and put in a series of smaller vessels with the same type of water. They can be fed on a proprietary brand of food such as Mikrocell, or on a suspension of yeast. The nauplii feed by filtering the tiny particles of food out of the water. Enough food should be added to make the water very slightly cloudy. As the larvae feed, the water becomes less cloudy, and when it is clear they can be given another small amount of the food. The principle here is little and often.

It is always advisable to feed fishes at the same time of day and in the same part of the tank. In most cases it will be sufficient to feed either in the morning or in the evening, and preferably in the morning as the fishes will then have the hours of light to feed in. Young fishes normally need to be fed several times a day, receiving only a small portion each time.

Apart from the various foods available from aquarium dealers there are some live foods which can be bred in boxes or small glass jars. In addition to brine shrimps *(Artemia)*, which have already been mentioned, these include the

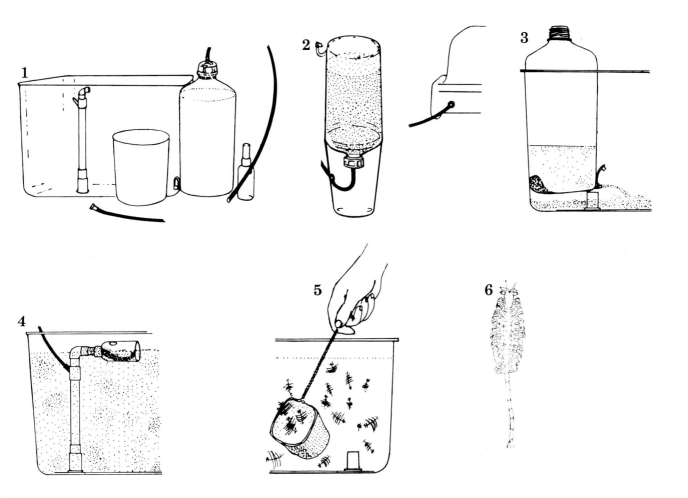

Diagram to show the hatching and rearing of brine shrimps
(Artemia)
1 the general equipment required
2 hatching the larvae from the eggs
3 transferring larvae to the rearing tank
4 introducing food (e.g. Mikrozell) for the larvae
5 removing adult brine shrimps for feeding to the fishes
6 an adult brine shrimp

small Grindal worms *(Enchytraeus buchholzi)* and microworms, which are even smaller, and of course whiteworms (up to 1 in long) and fruit-flies *(Drosophila)*. Many of these small animals are not aquatic, but some will live in the aquarium for quite a time: microworms about 6–8 hours, Grindal worms and whiteworms up to a week in fresh water. Incidentally, whiteworms should only be given as a supplementary food, perhaps twice a week. If fed too frequently the fish become fat and their readiness to spawn is impaired.

Mosquito and gnat larvae can be collected during the summer months from ponds or rain butts. They can be kept for a day or so in damp paper. If they are to be kept for more than a few days they should be put in stoppered tubes or jars. Although these larvae are an excellent food, there is always a chance that they may complete their development and emerge as troublesome gnats or mosquitoes.

The red earthworm *(Lumbricus rubellus)*, found under stones and fallen timber, is also very nutritious, but it is best not to use worms freshly collected from a compost heap, or the brandling worm *(Eisenia foetida)* as these may prove dangerous to the fishes.

Water-fleas can be kept in a cool place in shallow containers with the maximum surface area. If the dead ones are removed every day with a pipette and if the water is renewed every two days, it is possible to keep these tiny crustaceans over a long period. They will require feeding with very small amounts of fish meal or milk and they will also take any free-floating microscopic algae that are growing in the tank. When the fishes are breeding it is important to remove any water-fleas from the tank, as they multiply rapidly and may compete with the fish fry for infusorians and other microscopic foods.

Infusorians, as already mentioned, provide the smallest form of live food and are used to feed newly hatched young fishes. After hatching, most young fishes live for the first few days on the contents of their yolk sac, which forms a bulge below the body and hinders swimming. After two to three days the yolk sac contents will have been used up and the young fishes are then free-swimming. They now need a plentiful supply of very small food, which should be all round them, so that they only have to snap it up. At this time the depth of water in the tank can be reduced.

Infusorians should not be bred in the fish tank, but in a number of small glass vessels. A culture of *Paramecium* can be prepared by soaking hay, or preferably turnips, in rain or pond water, leaving the vessels in good light. After two to three days large numbers of *Paramecium* will have been produced, giving a pink colour to the culture. Small amounts of this liquid can then be transferred into the fish tank by a spoon or pipette. Only small amounts are recommended because *Paramecium* dies quite quickly in warm water. Portions of culture should be given several times a day.

Freeze-dried food is a fairly recent introduction in the aquarium world, but is proving very useful. Almost all kinds of food can be preserved by freeze-drying, and most fishes eat it very readily. Freeze-drying involves the removal of water from the tissue. It happens in winter when the washing is hanging out to dry in frosty weather. The clothes freeze and dry without dripping. The transition from ice to water vapour, without the intermediate liquid phase, is known as sublimation. This is the basic principle involved in freeze-drying. The process uses no heat, which would change the taste and value of the food, and no warm liquid, which would change its nature. The ice sublimes into water vapour which is blown away, leaving a light, porous mass. Only the water is removed, nothing else. This is still, of course, quite a costly process.

The different types of dried food are sold in the form of flakes or powder, and are best given in a feeding ring, a small ring floating at the surface which prevents the dried food from spreading. The fishes soon become aware of the presence of this food and quickly consume it. It will not attract most predatory fishes, but many of the cichlids will take it quite readily. Foods that are completely unsuitable for aquarium fishes include bread, rolls, cakes, biscuits, dried ants' pupae (erroneously known as ants' eggs), and cooked potatoes. Many of these cause intestinal disturbance and they all lead to pollution of the aquarium water.

Fish diseases

In common with all living organisms, fishes have certain defensive measures against the vectors, such as parasites, which cause disease. When, owing to some accident a fish becomes weakened, or conversely when a disease vector becomes stronger, symptoms of disease will often appear. This may be due to a number of external factors. It can happen for instance if a fish suffers injury when it is being caught and taken from its natural waters. In every case prevention is better than cure, although very often by the time the damage is noticed it may have progressed too far for a cure to be possible. The following points may be helpful:

1 Starvation and emaciation frequently lead to skin lesions, which are followed by fungal infections *(Saprolegnia)*.

2 Unsuitable food may cause intestinal disturbances. If the food contains too much fat, this will be deposited around the internal organs. If the diet is monotonous and low in vitamins there will be general debility and possibly liver degeneration. In general, it will do the fishes no harm to be kept very slightly hungry.

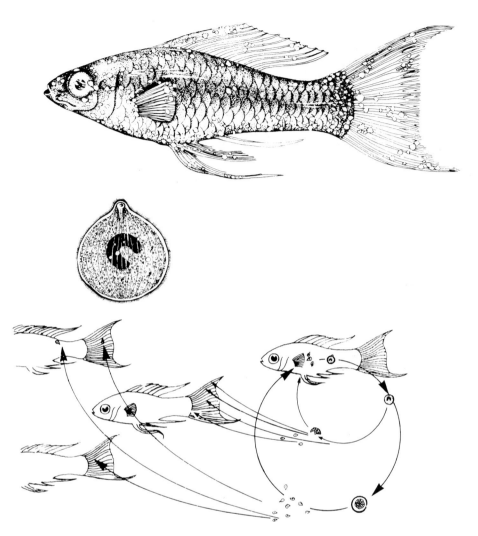

Life cycle of *Ichthyophthirius multifiliis* (white-spot). When adult, the spherical parasite on the skin of a fish falls to the bottom where it encysts. The contents of the cyst then divide to produce large numbers of motile spores which infect other fishes. At the top an infected fish. Below it is a much-enlarged drawing of the adult parasite showing the typical horseshoe-shaped nucleus

3   When the water temperature is too low the fishes become chilled and this usually leads to inflammation of the swimbladder and lowered resistance. Sudden excessive changes in the temperature are also to be avoided.

4   Lack of oxygen causes an increase in the rate of respiration and general debility.

5   Water that is too soft or with too low a pH does not suit all fishes. Those that live in coastal areas, such as some of the livebearers, will not tolerate very soft water or a low pH.

6   An excess of sunlight can also cause trouble, since in many cases it is associated with a rise in the pH to 10 or more, and this causes generalized cloudiness of the skin and frayed fins. The pH and hardness of the water should therefore be tested from time to time.

7   Injuries caused by apparatus or aggressive neighbours in the tank lead to infection of the wounds by bacteria or fungi.

8   Unsuitable materials used in the construction of the tank and technical equipment (e.g. metals, mastic, paint, tubing etc.) are often responsible for poisoning.

9   Injurious gases or vapours (e.g. from gas cookers, factory outlets, excessive tobacco smoke, insecticides etc.) may be sucked in by the air pump and thus reach the tank water.

This can be avoided by installing an air filter (with activated charcoal) between the pump and the diffuser, or by drawing in clean air from outside the room.

10 The remains of food left in the tank will decompose rapidly and lead to an accumulation of ammonia (which is poisonous), and of nitrates.

Steps must be taken to prevent the introduction of parasites and other disease vectors. Thus:

a Every new fish must undergo a period of quarantine before it is put into a community tank. All sick fishes must be kept separate from the others, until completely cured.

b It is dangerous to use live food, plants and water from ponds and streams unless these are known to be clean and free from disease.

c The substrate and all the rockwork must be thoroughly disinfected with potassium permanganate as some disease vectors have resistant spores, which can withstand heat and even desiccation.

d Nets, glass cleaners, tubing and feeding rings must be disinfected and carefully rinsed.

e Plants must be disinfected before being put into the tank and, of course, all rotting leaves should be removed.

f If a disease does break out, and the tank has to be emptied, it should be remembered that

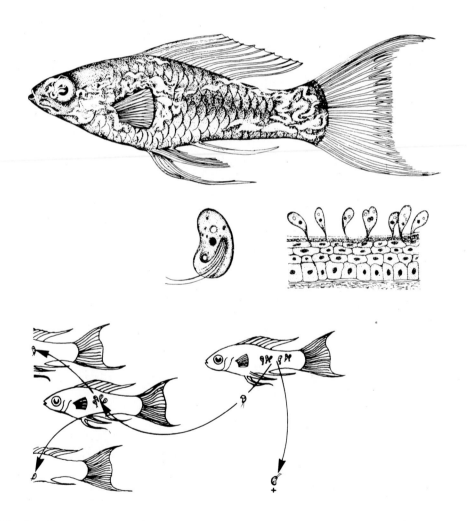

Transmission of the flagellate protozoan *Costia necatrix* is direct from the skin of one fish to the skin of another; the gills also become infected. The infected areas of skin become cloudy (see top drawing). Below this is a much enlarged drawing of a specimen of *Costia*, and to the right a drawing to show the way in which the parasites become attached to the skin everything in the tank must be thoroughly disinfected. This includes all equipment such as heaters, aerators and tubing, thermometer and filter.

These preventive measures should help in combatting disease. Sometimes, however, it becomes necessary to attempt a cure. This is mostly done to destroy external parasites. Internal diseases are rarely curable, largely because they are diagnosed too late. In a doubtful case one can tap the tank glass. If the fish is healthy it will react quickly and usually swim downwards. If, on the other hand, it is sick it will only swim away very slowly and rather irregu-

larly. If it rises towards the surface without fin movements or if it cannot get off the bottom without some difficulty, it is also likely to be ill. This also applies to fishes which stay below the surface and only move when pushed.

In general, the treatment of fish diseases by complicated drugs is not really a job for the home aquarist. His best course is first to take the precautions recommended above for avoiding the introduction of disease, and secondly to build up the resistance of his fishes, by providing them with water of the correct composition (hardness, pH) at the proper temperature, and by feeding them a balanced and varied diet.

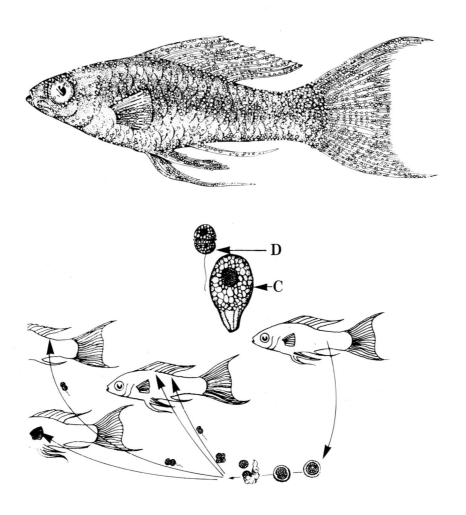

The life cycle of the dinoflagellate protozoan *Oodinium pillularis* is similar to that of *Ichthyophthirius*. The parasites develop on the skin and gills of a fish as tiny white spots, and when mature they fall to the bottom and encyst. Numerous divisions within the cyst (C) produce motile spores, here known as dinospores (D), and these infect other fishes

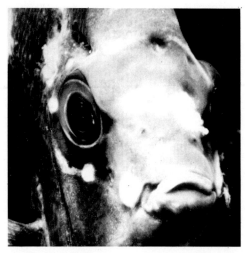

Head of a discus fish showing an advanced infection by *Hexamita (= Octomitus)*

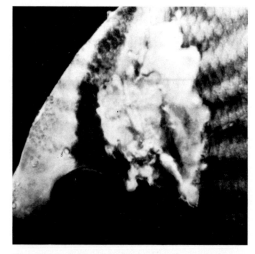

The final stage of a *Hexamita* infection

Lymphocystis, a virus infection in which small white nodules form on the skin

A dwarf gourami infected with *Ichthyophthirius* and with the ciliate *Hexamita*

A knifefish with white-spot *(Ichthyophthirius)*

A barb showing the tiny white nodules on skin and fins from *Oodinium pillularis*

Fish families and species

The family Pantodontidae (freshwater butterflyfishes)

This is what is known as a monotypic family, which means that it has only a single species, namely the butterflyfish *(Pantodon buchholzi)* of tropical West Africa, which grows to a length of about 10 cm (3¾ in). The shape of the body is somewhat unusual. The deeply cleft mouth faces upwards and the dorsal profile is almost a straight line, which indicates that this is a surface-living fish. In the wild, butterflyfishes live in quiet, flowing or standing waters rich in vegetation. They feed on insects at the water surface, but only rarely do they take insects in flight. When chasing an insect these fishes sometimes leave the water. The elongated pectoral (or breast) fins enable them to glide in the air for 1–2 m (c. 1–2 yards), while the ventral (or pelvic) fins help to provide a soft landing as they glide over the water before submerging.

In the aquarium these are peaceful, relatively hardy fishes when the water conditions are suitable. The water should not be hard (up to 8° DH), but slightly acid and the temperature at the surface should be 24–30°C (75–86°F). The diet can be insects and their larvae, and after a period of acclimatization freshly hatched mealworms and small fishes can also be offered. Butterflyfishes should not, therefore, be kept in a tank with smaller species that tend to live in the upper waters. The back of the tank can be decorated with rockwork and the foreground planted with long-stemmed vegetation with

Pantodon buchholzi

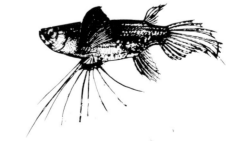

Pantodon buchholzi

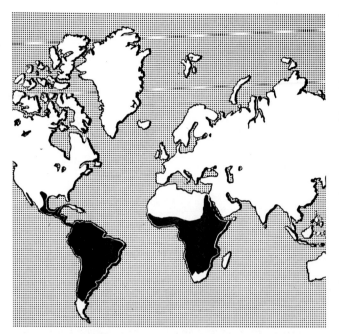

Distribution of the characin group

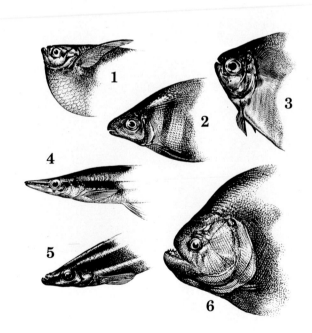

Studies of characin heads:
1 hatchetfish
2 *Distichodus*
3 *Metynnis*
4 *Phago*
5 headstander
6 piranha

leaves that lie on the water surface. With this amount of shade the fishes should spend the day near or at the surface and be fairly visible. The tank itself must be well covered to prevent the fishes gliding and ending up as dried specimens on the floor. Breeding is not easy. The anal fin is more deeply cleft in the male than in the female.

The family Characidae (characins)

This is a large family with over a thousand species from tropical and subtropical areas of Africa and America. Many popular aquarium fishes belonging to this family come from the enormous Amazon basin. These include the tetras in the genera *Hemigrammus* and *Hyphessobrycon*. The characins have no characteristic external features. Some are elongated, others disc-shaped, some have a short body, others an elongated head. The varied forms of the head and mouth are illustrated in the drawing and they relate, of course, to the way of life and feeding habits of the different species. All characins have teeth. In predatory characins, such as the piranhas, these may be very long. Most species have an adipose fin, a small, usually rayless fin lying between the dorsal and caudal fins. The brilliant colours are seen only when the conditions in the tank are correct. Characins usually require soft and slightly acid water. In the wild they live in quiet, flowing or standing waters with dense vegetation. They swim around in shoals, and the aquarist is therefore recommended not to buy just one or two individuals of a species as these seldom do well in captivity. The tank can have a few roots to provide suitable hiding-places.

In their natural environment characins have a rich and varied supply of food and this is probably a help to the aquarist, for in captivity these attractive fishes will usually eat almost anything they are offered. From time to time they should be given some live food.

The breeding of characins requires experience and a certain knowledge of biology and water chemistry. Most spawn at random in an aquarium, and this means that they lose all interest in their offspring after spawning and therefore do not practise any form of brood protection. The spawning tank should be fitted with a trap through which the eggs will fall so that they are

Pygocentrus piraya

A tank for characins, with a rock terrace in the background, plants and roots to provide shelter and open water for swimming in the foreground

out of the reach of the parent fishes, which would otherwise eat them. These traps can be easily constructed out of thin rods of plastic glued together with a suitable plastic glue and close enough to each other so that fishes cannot pass through. Among the numerous characin species the most notorious are the piranhas of South America, predatory fishes with long, sharp teeth, and many are the travellers' tales of how they reduce large mammals or even man to a skeleton in a remarkably short space of time. There are, in fact, four species to which this kind of reputation can be attached. These are the red piranha *(Serrasalmus nattereri)*, the piranha *(Pygocentrus piraya)*, the white

piranha *(Serrasalmus rhombeus)* and *Serrasalmus niger*. In nature these fishes move around in shoals, but in the home aquarium this may lead to trouble because the more aggressive individuals may injure the others, producing blood which will start the whole group on an orgy of cannibalism. In quite a short time only a small number of the more powerful specimens will survive.

Large species such as *Pygocentrus piraya* eventually reach a length of up to 60 cm (24 in). With adequate feeding such fishes will not grow too fast, even in a tank 120–150 cm (46–60 in) long. The tank should have a background of smooth rocks, of a type which will not leach

Moenkhausia sanctaefilomenae

The *Moenkhausia* species, which have characteristically large scales, will feed on almost anything, and if the tank has plants these should be tough varieties, otherwise they too will be eaten. There should be a few hiding-places and plenty of space for swimming. If kept in good condition the fishes can be transferred to a separate tank for breeding. The eggs are laid at random, but they may be eaten if the parents are not removed from the breeding tank.

The black tetra *(Gymnocorymbus ternetzi)* is a compressed, disc-shaped fish, up to about 5 cm (2 in) long. Several specimens should be kept together, and these would do well in a community tank. They are omnivorous and not

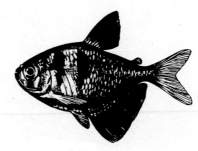

Gymnocorymbus ternetzi

calcareous material into the water. A few roots can be placed in the tank, and if possible, one or two tough plants, such as Java moss *(Vesicularia)*. The water should be soft (up to 8° DH) and slightly acid and the lighting subdued. These fishes require plenty of room for swimming, and they can be fed on *Tubifex* and mosquito larvae for small specimens and on fishes, lean meat (heart) and earthworms for larger individuals. The temperature in the middle water layers can fluctuate between 24° and 28°C (75–82°F).

The species of *Moenkhausia* come from South America. The glass tetra *(M. oligolepis)* grows up to 12 cm (4¾ in) in length, but is not kept so commonly as two other species which grow only to about half this length, namely *M. pittieri* and *M. sanctaefilomenae*. These are active but peaceful shoaling fishes, which do well in the community tank. They all have an adipose fin. They are not difficult to keep in soft water at a temperature of 22–26°C (72–79°F). Water with a hardness not exceeding 10° DH is normally recommended, but they seem to show no signs of suffering in water that is 5–6° harder. The water should be made slightly acid by filtration through peat, which should provide a pH of about 6.5.

difficult to breed, and so they are not very expensive to buy. The ground coloration is grey with black bars and there is a large black area covering the rear half of the body and the tail.

The X-ray fish *(Pristella riddlei)* is another active, omnivorous swarming fish, up to 5 cm (2 in) long, and with an adipose fin. It comes from northernmost South America. It should be kept in a tank with plenty of marginal vegetation and open water in the centre. This species

Pristella riddlei

Aphyocharax rubropinnis

Cheirodon axelrodi

Paracheirodon innesi

roots are ideal. The tank water should be slightly acid with a hardness of 12–16° DH. Tetras have been kept in water with a hardness of 16° DH, and they have grown from tiny newly imported young fishes to fully grown adults. It is important to keep them as a shoal of at least ten fishes, and as they are very tolerant they can be kept together with fishes belonging to other species.

The glowlight tetra *(Hemigrammus erythrozonus)* comes from northern South America and grows up to 5 cm (2 in) in length. It can be kept in a normal tank with some vegetation, and in soft, slightly acid water at a temperature of about 26°C (79°F). These are shoaling fishes which establish territories. They are not easy to breed, and in this context much depends upon the quality of the water.

Hemigrammus hyanuary, named after Lake Hyanuary in the Amazon basin, grows to 5 cm (2 in) and likes a tank with some plants and plenty of room for moving about. Very soft water is not necessary as it will live quite satisfactorily in water with a hardness of 10–12° DH, but a proportion should be changed at regular intervals. The temperature should lie between 24 and 26°C (76–79°F). These are omnivorous fishes, which can be kept in a community tank, and they can be bred.

can be bred. During the spawning period the caudal fin of the male is considerably redder than that of the female. These fishes require the same water conditions as the preceding species.

The bloodfin *(Aphyocharax rubropinnis)* comes from Argentina and the neighbouring Rio Paraná. This is a hardy omnivorous fish, growing up to 6 cm (2¼ in) long, which lives for quite a time in the aquarium. It should be kept in a spacious tank with plenty of vegetation. The water can have a hardness of 8–12° DH and a temperature of 22–28°C (72–82°F), but an occasional drop to 18°C (64°F) will do no harm.

Most of the species in the genera *Hemigrammus* and *Hyphessobrycon* come from South America, with a few from Central America. These include some of the most popular small aquarium fishes. The majority have an angular and often tall dorsal fin. The group includes the neon tetra *(Paracheirodon innesi)* and the cardinal tetra *(Cheirodon axelrodi)*. In general, all the small tetras require similar aquarium conditions. The tank should have sufficient marginal vegetation and a reasonable amount of open water for swimming. Naturally there should be a certain amount of cover, and for this a few

Hemigrammus erythrozonus

Hyphessobrycon callistus callistus

Hyphessobrycon ornatus

Petitella georgiae comes from the waters of the upper Amazon, and never exceeds 5 cm (2 in) in length. It is somewhat more difficult to keep

Petitella georgiae

than the preceding species, and is not known to have bred in the aquarium. It likes soft, acid water at a temperature of about 24°C (75°F).

Several of the species of *Hyphessobrycon* are suitable for the home aquarium, and some are very attractive. These include the blood characin or jewel tetra (*Hyphessobrycon callistus*), the bleeding heart tetra *(H. rubrostigma)* as well as *H. 'roberti'* and *H. ornatus*. These are all easy to keep in the aquarium, but not so easy to breed. The sexes can be distinguished quite readily, for the males usually have brighter colours and the females are much stouter. For these characins the tank should have a minimum length of 40 cm (16 in), and the water should be soft and slightly acid, at a temperature of 24°C (75°F). There should be sufficient hiding-places and enough space for swimming. A proportion of the water should be changed at frequent intervals and the fishes offered as much live food as possible.

The blind cave characin (*Astyanax jordani*), which grows to a length of 7 cm ($2\frac{3}{4}$ in), comes from underground waters in the cave area of the Rio Panuco at San Luis Potosi in Mexico.

Hyphessobrycon rubrostigma

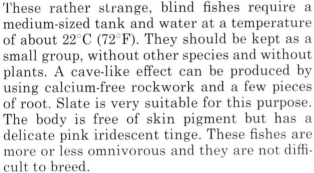

Hyphessobrycon 'roberti' (above) and *H. ornatus* (below)

Astyanax jordani

These rather strange, blind fishes require a medium-sized tank and water at a temperature of about 22°C (72°F). They should be kept as a small group, without other species and without plants. A cave-like effect can be produced by using calcium-free rockwork and a few pieces of root. Slate is very suitable for this purpose. The body is free of skin pigment but has a delicate pink iridescent tinge. These fishes are more or less omnivorous and they are not difficult to breed.

Ephippicharax orbicularis comes from the rivers of eastern South America that flow into the Atlantic Ocean, its distribution range extending from Guyana to the Rio Grande do Sul and Paraguay. It can grow up to 12 cm (4¾ in) in length. This is a very suitable shoaling fish for the beginner aquarist, being peaceful and hardy. The tank can have a capacity of 80 litres (18 gallons) and the water should be medium-hard and at a temperature of about 24°C (75°F). The substrate should not be too pale. These fishes require space for swimming in the centre of the tank, but a few tough, broad-leaved plants such as *Echinodorus* (the Amazon sword plant) can

Ephippicharax orbicularis

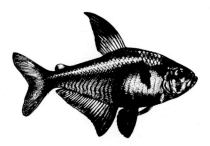

Megalamphodus sweglesi

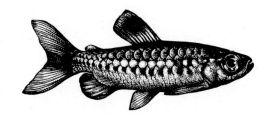

Arnoldichthys spilopterus

be put round the edges, and some floating plants will help to give a subdued light. The fishes are omnivorous and will eat plants with tender leaves. Another rather smaller omnivorous species from the Amazon basin is *Megalamphodus sweglesi*, which is not at all difficult to keep. It grows to a length of about 4.5 cm (1¾ in) and has attractive red coloration.

The African characins are just as beautiful as their South American relatives, but they are rather different in appearance, having a more elongated body and strikingly large scales. The best known are the red-eyed characin *(Arnoldichthys spilopterus)*, the Congo tetra *(Micralestes interruptus)*, the long-finned characin *(Alestes longipinnis)* and *A. chaperi*. They all come from West Africa. The largest is *A. longipinnis* which reaches a length of 14 cm (5½ in), the smallest *M. interruptus* (8 cm or 3 in). The females are normally smaller than the males. The tank for these fishes can be set up in the same way as for the South American characins, leaving plenty of space for swimming. This is particularly important in the case of *M. interruptus* in which the fins will only reach their full development if the fishes are not cramped for space. It is possible, but not easy, to breed some of the African characins.

Micralestes interruptus

Headstanders

These fishes, forming the family Anostomidae, are so called because they normally swim head downwards. This is an adaptation to life in their home waters where they remain in this vertical position among plants with long, narrow leaves. They require a tank with a length of at least 100 cm (39 in) and a varied diet of animal food with some plant material. The small mouth at the tip of the muzzle is used to graze algae off the plants and also to pick up worms from the bottom.

Alestes longipinnis

Anostomus anostomus

The most commonly kept headstander, and perhaps the most beautiful, is the striped anostomus *(Anostomus anostomus)*, a species best kept as a small shoal. Here the mouth is at the tip of the muzzle but it faces slightly upwards, owing to the elongation of the lower jaw. This means that when picking food up from the bottom the fish not only stands on its head, but literally leans over backwards.

The spotted headstander *(Chilodus punctatus)* which is up to 7–8 cm (2¾–3 in) long should be kept as a shoal in a tank that is at least 80 cm (32 in) long. If the tank is too cramped the fishes may jump out, and this usually means their death. These fishes are rather difficult to acclimatize, and they do not like a change of water, but if they survive this period, they may live for several years. They spend more or less the whole day looking for food, and are not very demanding. The sexes are difficult to distinguish, although the male usually has a longer dorsal fin.

Other species sometimes kept in the aquarium include the headstander *(Abramites microcephalus)*, the three-spot anostomus *(Anostomus trimaculatus)* and *Leporinus affinis*. Of these *Leporinus* is really only suitable for a home aquarium when it is quite young, as it grows eventually to a length of 30 cm (12 in), feeding almost exclusively on plants, including those intended for decoration. The other two species only reach a length of about 15 cm (6 in) and they do not grow so fast as the *Leporinus*, so they are more suitable for the home aquarium. If given a regular supplement of lettuce leaves or other greenstuff they will not attack the aquarium plants, which would normally be sword plants of the genus *Echinodorus*.

Nannostomus trifasciatus

Chilodus punctatus

Pencilfishes

These remarkably slender fishes are similar in many respects to the true characins. The scientific name of the family, Hemiodontidae, means 'half-toothed', and refers to the fact that these fishes only have teeth in the upper jaw. The family includes several beautiful and popular aquarium fishes, all from South America. These include *Poecilobrycon harrisoni (=Nannostomus harrisoni)*, the three-banded pencilfish *(N. trifasciatus)* and the one-lined pencilfish *Poecilobrycon unifasciatus (=N. unifasciatus)*, all about 6 cm ($2\frac{1}{4}$ in) long. There are several other species, some of which have subspecies.

Pencilfishes can be kept in a tank with dense marginal vegetation and some roots to provide cover. They mostly remain more or less motionless among the plants and are not very active swimmers, although if threatened they can react very rapidly. The substrate should be dark, as it is in their home range, and the water must be soft, filtered through peat, and kept at a temperature of 24–26°C (75–79°F). Pencilfishes should be fed as much as possible on live food, preferably insect larvae, although this is not always possible.

Poecilobrycon harrisoni

The habitat of *Anostomus* and *Poecilobrycon* on the Rio Cucuçamba, north of Obidos in the central Amazon region

Poecilobrycon unifasciatus

The family Citharinidae

These characin-type fishes all come from Africa, and they are characterized by the straight lateral line. The genus *Distichodus* contains a number of rather plump fishes which live in a shoal and grow quite large, so they require a really spacious tank. The one usually kept is the six-banded distichodus *(Distichodus sexfasciatus)*, which will eventually grow in a large tank to a length of up to 25 cm (9¾ in), which is much too big for the average home aquarium. It can, however, be a good aquarium fish when quite young, at a length of 8–10 cm (3–3¾ in). It should be given a diet of animal food with a supplement of plant material. It is, however, possible that it switches to a more vegetarian diet at night, so it may be a good idea to provide a variety of plant food such as lettuce, boiled spinach, algae (taken from other tanks) and oatflakes, in addition to

Distichodus sexfasciatus

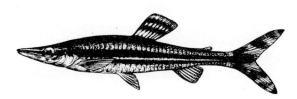

Phago loricatus

the usual live food (*Tubifex*, water-fleas, insect larvae). The genus *Citharinus* contains similarly built fishes, but they are too large, and the aquarist should not be tempted to buy them.

One other member of this group may be mentioned, namely *Phago loricatus*, which comes from the River Niger in West Africa and grows to a length of 15 cm (6 in). This is a rather shy species, which requires a tank with plenty of vegetation and fairly subdued light. The water can be medium-hard, but it must be kept warm, at about 28°C (82°F). The sides of the body are a delicate rust-brown with two or three narrow, dark longitudinal stripes. The transparent fins have a yellowish sheen. The dorsal fin is marked with two dark bars and the caudal fin also has dark markings. *Phago* is certainly a handsome fish for the aquarium, but it raises problems, as it will only eat live food (small fishes and insect larvae) and needless to say it cannot be kept with other species. It is not known to have bred in the aquarium.

Hatchetfishes

These characin-like fishes have for some time been classified in their own family, the Gasteropelecidae. They come from the area between Panama and southern Brazil, living mainly in small tributaries of the larger rivers. The dorsal profile is almost straight, but the ventral side of the body is characteristically arched, giving it a very unusual appearance. With the help of the sail-like pectoral fins and strong muscles, hatchetfishes are able to leave the water and glide over the surface for distances of 3–5 m (c. 3–5 yards).

Hatchetfishes range in size from the tiny *Carnegiella myersi*, only 2.5 cm (1 in) long, through *C. strigata*, the marbled hatchetfish shown here, to *Thoracocharax securis* which reaches a length of 9 cm ($3\frac{1}{2}$ in). These fishes are not really suitable for the beginner. They require a tank with a large surface area and a close-fitting lid, otherwise they literally take off and fall to the floor. The tank vegetation should include some plants with long stalks and large leaves that lie on the water surface. The fishes will seek shelter beneath these leaves against attacks from above. The tank water ought to be soft, slightly acid and with a temperature at the surface of 25–30°C (77–86°F). In the wild, hatchetfishes hunt their prey at the water surface, living mainly on insects and their larvae, but in the aquarium they will also take small crustaceans. Several of the hatchetfishes have been bred by aquarists, but there is evidently little information available on this subject. It is very difficult, in fact almost impossible, to distinguish the sexes. Hatchetfishes do quite well in a community tank with species that prefer the middle and lower water layers.

Barbs

This family, the Cyprinidae, has a very wide distribution, and it contains a large number of species that are suitable for the home aquarium. These include the danios, the rasboras and the true barbs, which are here classified in the genus *Barbus* rather than *Puntius*, a name which has sometimes been used. The family also includes several coldwater species such as carp, tench, chub, minnow and goldfish.

Carnegiella strigata strigata and *C. s. vesca*

Distribution of the carp and barb family (Cyprinidae)

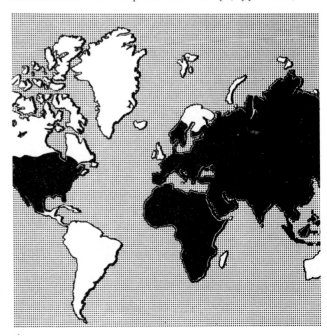

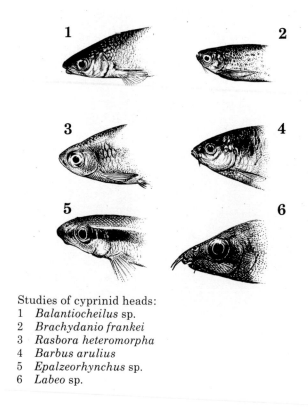

Studies of cyprinid heads:
1 *Balantiocheilus* sp.
2 *Brachydanio frankei*
3 *Rasbora heteromorpha*
4 *Barbus arulius*
5 *Epalzeorhynchus* sp.
6 *Labeo* sp.

Many of the *Barbus* species are quite easy to breed in the aquarium, often producing large broods. As a result these are relatively inexpensive aquarium fishes. The parent fishes tend to eat the eggs, so the breeding tank must be furnished with a spawning trap or with small glass balls on the bottom so that the eggs can fall into the spaces between them.

The danios also are excellent for the home aquarium and very suitable for the beginner, and will live and feed readily in water kept at a temperature of 20–24°C (68–75°F). When fed properly they will breed just as readily as the species of *Barbus*. The rasboras from Malaysia and the Sunda Islands are also not difficult to keep, but not so easy to breed. They are more demanding as regards the composition of the water. Several other tropical cyprinids will be described in the following pages, but here it seems appropriate to make some mention of the best known of all the Cyprinidae, namely the goldfish *(Carassius auratus)*. At one time it was fashionable to keep one or two goldfish in a spherical bowl, a most unsuitable container for any aquatic animal. Some aquarists keep ordinary goldfishes in an outside pond, but the cult of this species has given rise to specialists,

Most, but not all, members of the family have one or two pairs of barbels on the lips. These carry sensory tissue which helps the fishes to find food on the bottom. The mouth can be protruded when feeding. Cyprinid fishes do not have an adipose fin, with very few exceptions.

Tropical barbs kept in the aquarium come primarily from south-east Asia and Africa, many living in shallow water with a moderate rate of flow. They are mostly shoaling fishes, so are best kept several together. They have no special requirements as regards the composition of the water, but it should be filtered. They spend the day swimming around in search of food, not despising algae, and they are particularly active when live food is offered. They will also, however, eat dried, freeze-dried and deep-frozen (but thawed) foods.

Veiltail goldfish

Veiltail goldfish, different varieties

originally in China and Japan but now world-wide, who have produced a vast assemblage of fancy goldfishes, known under such names as veiltails, telescope-eyes, lion-heads and so on.

Goldfishes are really coldwater animals, and although they will tolerate higher temperatures, they are best kept in tanks in water not exceeding 15°C (59°F). They swim about more or less continuously, eat anything they can find, including the aquarium plants, and their activities tend to stir up any detritus present, so the tank water should be filtered continuously. The fancy

Brachydanio albolineatus

Balantiocheilus melanopterus

which must have a close-fitting lid as these fishes tend to jump, can be furnished with a suitable arrangement of rocks and roots. A few plants can be used, provided they are robust, as the fishes like to bite pieces out of them. These fishes are not particularly demanding as regards the quality of the water, but they will do best in soft to medium-hard water (12–16° DH), with a slightly acid pH and at a temperature of 24–26°C (75–79°F). They will eat all types of food. Evidently *Balantiocheilus* has not yet been bred in captivity, and so all aquarium specimens have to be imported, and this naturally means that they may be quite expensive to buy.

The danios can rightly be regarded as highly satisfactory fishes for the home aquarium. They provide almost everything that the aquarist wants: brilliant coloration, small size, liveliness, hardiness, and last but not least they are not too difficult to breed. Five species are particularly suitable for the aquarium. These are the leopard danio (*Brachydanio frankei*), the pearl danio (*B. albolineatus*), the spotted danio (*B. nigrofasciatus*), the zebra danio (*B. rerio*) and the giant danio (*Danio malabaricus*). The last named species grows to a length of 15 cm (6 in), but the others only up to about 6 cm (2¼ in). These small fishes, whose coloration is predominantly blue, are very active swimmers, always on the search for food. They do well in a

forms are not so hardy as the original goldfishes, and some of them are sensitive to drastic changes of the tank water.

One of the most striking of the tropical barbs is *Balantiocheilus melanopterus*, which comes from south-east Asia, including the Greater Sunda Islands. These fishes will do well if kept as a small shoal in a fairly large tank, at least 80 cm (32 in) for young specimens. As they grow they will need to be transferred to a larger tank, and if they have sufficient space they will eventually reach a length of 25 cm (10 in). The tank,

A tank for barbs, furnished with flat rocks, a soft substrate, several species of *Cryptocoryne* and a few floating plants

Danio malabaricus

Brachydanio frankei

community tank, which can be furnished with some tall vegetation round the edges, and with roots and a few rocks in the centre. These species are not very sensitive to hard water. The average temperature of the tank water should be about 23°C (73°F), but this can be allowed to drop a few degrees during the winter months. The health of the fishes will suffer if the water is colder than 18°C (64°F). The tank should not be too dimly lit. There should be no trouble about feeding, as they will take almost anything.

It is not too difficult to distinguish the sexes when the fishes are sexually mature. The females are usually a little larger than the males and their belly is stouter and more convex. A tank 30–40 cm (12–15 in) long is sufficient for breeding, and it should have some plants with feathery leaves in one corner, but not too much light. Plants are not always necessary in the case of the zebra danio. The female should be placed in the tank first and given a day in which to acclimatize, before introducing two males. If it is at all possible the aquarist should try to watch the spawning process, and as soon as it has finished he must take all the fishes from the tank. If this is not done the parents will eat the eggs. At a temperature of about 26°C (79°F) the eggs develop rapidly and should hatch after about twenty-four hours. The young are not

Brachydanio rerio

Brachydanio nigrofasciatus

very difficult to rear. The same adults can be put together again after about a month.

Two species of *Epalzeorhynchus* are also kept in the aquarium. These are *E. kalopterus* and *E. siamensis*, and both come from south-east Asia. The mouth is positioned ventrally and has thick lips, the upper lip being much enlarged. This sucker-like mouth enables the fishes to rasp algae and also to attach themselves to roots and stones in the often fast-flowing rivers of their home waters. They are good swimmers and a small shoal makes an attractive sight. When properly cared for they should live for several years and may grow up to a length of 10 cm (3¾ in).

The aquarist can use these fishes to keep his tank free of algae; a job which they do remarkably well. *E. kalopterus* has been known for a long time, but *E. siamensis* was not discovered until the end of the '50s, and it has proved to be the more efficient consumer of algae. Unlike *E. kalopterus* it appears to be something of a lone wolf, and becomes very aggressive if the tank contains too many individuals of its own species. On the other hand, it does not worry other species, so a single specimen makes a good addition to a community tank.

These two species can be kept in a tank with dense vegetation, in water at a temperature of

Epalzeorhynchus kalopterus

23–26°C (73–79°F). They have proved very hardy in a wide variety of aquarium conditions and appear to have no special requirements. They are said to tolerate being transferred from rain water poor in mineral salts to hard, mains water with a high content of salts. As they are primarily bottom-living fishes the tank should be provided with sufficient hiding-places. Like loaches they will often support themselves on the pectoral fins when at rest. It is scarcely possible to distinguish the sexes on external features, and these two species have not yet been bred in captivity.

The species of the genus *Labeo* also live mainly on or near the bottom. The genus contains some rather large species, but for the home aquarium there are smaller, attractive forms. One of the best known is the red-tailed 'shark' *Labeo bicolor*, and occasionally dealers may have the related *L. frenatus*, which has somewhat paler coloration, without the sharp contrast. The popular use of the term 'shark' is very misleading as these fishes are in no way related to the true sharks, which are of course cartilaginous fishes. The lips have small horny papillae which are used to rasp algae from rocks and roots in the oxygen-saturated, fast-flowing small rivers of south-east Asia. The elongated,

Labeo bicolor

torpedo-like shape of the body and the very large caudal fin help the fishes to escape rapidly to shelter when threatened. Many aquarists will have experienced the speed and swimming efficiency of these fishes when trying to catch them up in an aquarium tank. They can indeed swim in almost any body position. They are often upside down when grazing algae off the underside of leaves and, particularly when young, they may take up a vertical position in the water and clean algae off the tank glass. At other times, rather like some of the catfishes, they use the pectoral fins to drag themselves along the bottom, like little seals.

They do not do well in hard water, and will not then show their full coloration. They should, in fact, be kept in soft, acid water, preferably filtered through peat, at a temperature of 24–26°C (75–79°F), and many aquarists find that it is a good idea to renew a proportion of this every three to four weeks. They may be regarded as omnivorous, but if there is not much algal growth in the tank they should be given a supplement of greenstuff (lettuce).

Labeo frenatus

As they grow older these fishes may become very aggressive. When a so-called pair is purchased it will often be found that the individuals grow at different rates. This is partly due to hereditary factors and the difference may become increasingly apparent as the fishes grow. It has often been found that aggressive behaviour starts when a group of young specimens is put into a tank. To a certain extent it can be avoided by keeping only a few individuals of one species in a large tank (upwards of 100 cm (39 in) long) and by providing suitable decoration, roots, rocks and vegetation to divide up the area so that the fishes can establish separate territories. If this kind of arrangement cannot be provided it is much better to keep only a single specimen in a tank.

The two species of *Labeo* just discussed grow relatively slowly and seldom, if ever, reach their maximum size of 20 cm (7¾ in) in an aquarium tank. It is otherwise with the so-called black 'shark' *(Morulius chrysophekadion)*. This species is quite attractive when young, but it grows very rapidly and may reach a length of 60 cm (23 in) so it is not really suitable for a home aquarium.

The genus *Barbus* contains a large number of species, known as barbs, many of which have become very popular. (These fishes are sometimes classified in the genus *Puntius* but the name *Barbus* is preferable.) On account of the large number of barbs it would be quite impossible to include them all.

One of the best of these is *Barbus arulius* from south-east Asia, which grows to a length of 12 cm (4¾ in). These fishes should be kept as a small shoal, but they have a tendency to nibble the softer parts of plants and also the more delicate fins of some other fishes. They require a medium-hard water at a temperature of about 24°C (75°F), and they can be bred. The back is an iridescent green, the flanks silvery and the outer edges of the caudal and anal fins are red. In the male the rays of the dorsal fin are much elongated.

The Angola barb *(B. barilioides)* comes from tropical West Africa (Angola). These are active fishes, which should not be kept in a tank that is too small, for they need plenty of space for swimming if they are to thrive. When swimming around, the shoal may stop for a short rest, often in among dense vegetation, so the tank can have plants round the edges. These fishes do not like too much light, and if the tank lighting cannot be easily regulated, as is often the case, an adequate amount of shade can be provided by having a few plants with broad, floating leaves. The water should be soft to medium-hard, at approximately pH 7, and at a temperature not less than 23°C (73°F). This is an omnivorous species, which has not yet been bred in captivity.

Barbus conchonius

The rosy barb *(Barbus conchonius)*, on the other hand, is relatively easy to breed. It comes from the eastern part of the Indian sub-continent, and is undoubtedly one of the most beautiful aquarium fishes. The coloration of the female is always somewhat paler than that of the male. During the spawning period the male is a brilliant red colour with a deep black marking on each side just in front of the caudal peduncle. In both sexes the scales are strikingly large. Rosy barbs should be kept in a tank set up as for *B. barilioides*, but as they like to dig, the substrate should be fine and not too pale. It is important to keep the substrate clean by siphoning off and washing the upper layer from time to time. In the natural range of the species the water is always clear.

Barbus conchonius

top: *Barbus lateristriga*
above: *Barbus arulius*

Barbus barilioides

As already mentioned, breeding is not only possible, but also very productive. In fact, this is one of the easiest barbs to breed. The parent fishes will, however, try to eat the eggs so they must be removed from the tank as soon as the spawning process has finished. Rosy barbs become sexually mature at a length of 6 cm ($2\frac{1}{4}$ in) but they can grow larger.

The spanner barb *(Barbus lateristriga)* is somewhat longer, up to about 20 cm ($7\frac{3}{4}$ in). It comes from Malaya and the Greater and Lesser Sunda Islands, and has a very striking pattern on the sides of the body. The ground coloration is fairly pale and this, together with its relatively large size, somewhat restricts its distribution in the aquarium world. The fins are transparent. Spanner barbs are active fishes, and in spite of their size they are peaceful and do well as a shoal. They like plenty of space for swimming and the marginal vegetation should consist of large, tough plants. They are omnivorous

Barbus nigrofasciatus

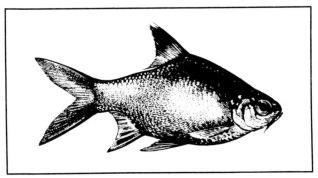

Barbus schwanenfeldi

and should be kept in medium-hard water at a temperature of about 23°C (73°F).

A smaller member of the barb group is the black ruby *(Barbus nigrofasciatus)*, which grows to a length of about 6 cm (2¼ in) and comes from Ceylon (Sri Lanka). These active little fishes can be bred and easily reared. They require a medium-hard water at a somewhat higher temperature (26°C or 79°F) than most of the other barbs.

The slightly smaller island barb *(Barbus oligolepis)*, reaches a length of 5 cm (2 in) at the most, and comes from south-east Asia (Sumatra). Island barbs are very suitable fishes for the beginner aquarist and they can be bred. They require water with a hardness of 10–15° DH, kept at a temperature of about 23°C (73°F). They do well as a small shoal and the tank should not have too much vegetation.

Schwanenfeld's barbs *(Barbus schwanenfeldi)* are considerably larger and only suitable for the

home aquarium when young, for they can grow up to 35 cm (13¾ in) in length. These are handsome, orange-coloured fishes with large scales, the coloration being particularly brilliant on the ventral and anal fins. The outer part of the deeply cleft caudal fin is black, edged with a thin orange stripe. This species should be kept as a shoal and is most likely to be seen in a public aquarium. Single specimens can be kept, but tend to become rather aggressive. Schwanenfeld's barbs seem always to be hungry and they can sometimes be seen, head down, digging in the substrate, and the sensory barbels must play a part in this activity. They will eat almost anything, but require a certain amount of plant food in their diet. If this is not provided they will vigorously attack the aquarium plants, particularly those with feathery leaves. In any case the plants must be well rooted in the bottom, otherwise the powerful fin movements of the fishes will soon tear them out. These fishes should only be kept together with other large species. The tank water, which must not be soft, should be kept at a temperature of about 24°C (75°F).

The Sumatra or tiger barb *(Barbus tetrazona)* must be one of the best known of all aquarium fishes, with its beautiful black, yellow and red coloration. These are easy fishes to breed in the aquarium, producing large numbers of offspring, and this has, of course, helped to keep the market price at a reasonable level. They live mainly in shoals which develop a distinct hierarchy or 'pecking order', a phenomenon which occurs in many animal groups. The tank should have plenty of space for swimming, and marginal vegetation with tough plants. A few tree roots will help to divide up the space. Sumatra barbs should never be kept together with species that have long fins, as they are very likely to nibble these.

below: *Barbus oligolepis*

above: *Barbus tetrazona*

Typical barb habitat in south-east Asia

A somewhat smaller species is the cherry barb *(Barbus titteya)* which grows to a length of about 5 cm (2 in). This is not such a robust fish and rapidly becomes timid when kept with species that are too aggressive. The coloration is a delicate rust-brown, showing greenish iridescence in certain lights. The gill covers and all the fins are bright red. Cherry barbs are active swimmers which prefer medium-hard water and a temperature of 24–26°C (75–79°F). They breed well in the aquarium, often producing large numbers of offspring.

The rasboras, almost all of which come from south-east Asia, also belong to the barb family and they have similar requirements to the

Barbus titteya

species just discussed. The popular harlequin fish *(Rasbora heteromorpha)* belongs here. It grows to a length of 4.5 cm ($1\frac{3}{4}$ in), whereas the rather similar Hengel's rasbora *(Rasbora hengeli)* is smaller (up to 3 cm or $1\frac{1}{4}$ in). Both these species prefer soft water (below 8° DH) and a slightly acid to acid pH. Some aquarists regard them as being rather difficult to keep. However, if sensitive fishes such as these are transferred from the soft water of a dealer's tank to mains water with a hardness of 18–20° DH it is not surprising that the casualty rate will rise.

The tank in which these fishes are kept should have dense marginal vegetation with fine-leaved plants, which thrive better in soft water than in hard. Rasboras prefer a really dark substrate and dim lighting. Some small floating plants, such as *Riccia*, will provide good shade. These rasboras can be kept in a community tank with others of a similar size. They like a temperature around 24°C (75°F) and although they will eat almost anything, they prefer live food to dried.

It is not always easy to distinguish the sexes in *R. heteromorpha* and *R. hengeli*. In the somewhat larger and stouter female the front edge of the wedge-shaped marking is straight, whereas in the more slender male it is rounded. These species can be bred, and here it is particularly important that the water should be soft.

The scissors-tail *(Rasbora trilineata)* also comes from south-east Asia (Malaya, Sumatra,

below: *Rasbora trilineata*

above: *Rasbora heteromorpha*

Borneo). These are active shoaling fishes which reach a length of up to 15 cm (6 in) and live for quite a long time. They will not, however, reach this size if kept in a medium-sized tank (up to 70 cm or 27 in long). They are omnivorous and their requirements are in general similar to those of the two preceding species, but they are more hardy, and they do not need such dim lighting.

Other rasboras kept in the home aquarium include the slender rasbora *(Rasbora daniconius)* which grows to 10 cm (3¾ in) long; the eyespot rasbora *(R. dorsiocellata)*, about 7 cm (2¾ in) long; the very beautiful *R. kalochroma*, up to 12 cm (4¾ in) long, and the similarly sized elegant rasbora *(R. lateristriata)*. There are also some much smaller species, such as the spotted rasbora *(R. maculata)*, only 2.5 cm (1 in) long, and *R. urophthalma* which is about the same size. Rasboras can all be kept in the same way, but not all of them have been bred in the aquarium.

The mormyrid family

The mormyrids are often known as elephant-trunk fishes from the shape of the mouth which in many species is elongated to form a proboscis. They are neither too delicate nor too demanding in their requirements. The temperature near the bottom should be kept as close as possible to 24°C (75°F), and a proportion of the water should be renewed at intervals. Newly purchased specimens should be kept in water that has stood for a long time or in an aquarium that has been in use. The substrate should be soft and dark.

Mormyrids feed mainly on small worms, and on the whole it is not a good idea to keep several specimens of the same species in a tank. They

Head of a mormyrid

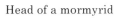

Rasbora dorsiocellata

Rasbora kalochroma

Rasbora lateristriata

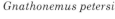

Gnathonemus petersi

Rasbora maculata

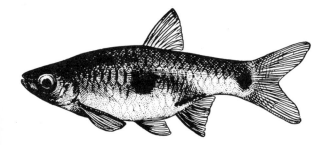

Rasbora urophthalma

A tank for loaches with rocks and roots arranged to provide shelter, with plants of *Cryptocoryne* and plenty of space for swimming

Heads of certain bottom-living fishes:

1 *Gyrinocheilus aymonieri*   2   a loach

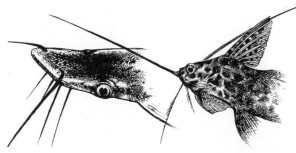

3   *Sorubim lima*   4   a pimelodid catfish

5   an armoured catfish   6   a loricariid catfish

produce electric pulses, and it is possible that they disturb one another. Two of the species commonly imported are *Gnathonemus moorii* and *G. petersi*, and these are not too difficult to keep. They require a spacious, covered tank with sufficient hiding-places (rockwork, roots), fairly dense marginal vegetation, and dim lighting, as these are fishes of the twilight. The water must be as soft as possible, and should be kept at a temperature in the range 22–28°C (72–82°F), depending on the conditions the fishes have previously experienced. Although they prefer small worms, they can be acclimatized to take other kinds of food. Mormyrids grow relatively fast and in a spacious tank they may exceptionally reach a length of 20 cm ($7\frac{3}{4}$ in). They will establish territories in the tank, and the weaker individuals will tend to be bullied.

The family Gyrinocheilidae

Gyrinocheilus aymonieri is the only species in the family Gyrinocheilidae, and one which is popular with aquarists because it is such an efficient consumer of algal growths. One or two of these fishes will, in fact, keep the algae in a tank within reasonable limits. When moving about they prefer to keep close to the bottom, and they frequently attach themselves by the suctorial mouth to rocks and also to the tank glass. When

Gyrinocheilus aymonieri

Acanthophthalmus kuhlii

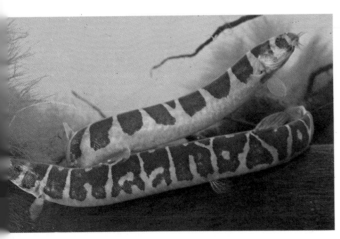

Acanthophthalmus sp.

attached in this way they obviously cannot take water into the mouth for respiratory purposes, but they have developed an additional opening just above each gill opening, through which water for respiration reaches the gills.

In south-east Asia *Gyrinocheilus* lives mainly in fast-flowing streams, and reaches a length of up to 25 cm (9¾ in), but it never grows so large in an aquarium tank. In addition to algae it also feeds on live food in the streams. In the aquarium it likes clear water rich in oxygen, at a temperature between 20° and 28°C (68–82°F). So far as is known there are no external differences between the sexes, and the species has not been bred in the aquarium. *Gyrinocheilus* does not damage aquarium plants, even when removing algae from them, but care should be taken when keeping this species together with large, disc-shaped fishes, as it sometimes tries to attach itself to them by suction. This causes injury and loss of scales. With increasing age *Gyrinocheilus* may become very aggressive.

The loach family

The loach family (Cobitidae) contains a number of sociable fishes which do well in the aquarium. They have a ventrally positioned mouth with which they graze algae from rocks and roots, but their main diet consists of worms, insect larvae and other small invertebrates. In front of each eye there is an erectile spine which can inflict a painful wound on the hand when one is trying to catch them. They come to the surface to swallow air which passes down the alimentary tract to the hindgut which has thin walls richly supplied with blood vessels. Here the oxygen is extracted from the air, and the residual gas is passed out at the anus. This method of respiration enables loaches to live in waters that are deficient in oxygen. As far as is known tropical loaches do not appear to have been bred in captivity.

Loaches for the tropical aquarium all come from south-east Asia. These include several species in the genus *Acanthophthalmus*, such as *A. semicinctus*, *A. kuhlii* and *A. myersi*, which are known as coolie loaches; they reach a length of about 8 cm (3 in). These fishes are active in the twilight hours, and usually spend the day hidden away; the tank lighting should be adjusted

89

to allow for this. The substrate should be soft and dark, and the tank can also be furnished with well-washed roots and non-calcareous rocks, as well as some dense vegetation, at least round the edges. Coolie loaches require soft water, with a hardness not exceeding 10° DH, kept at a temperature of 24–28°C (75–82°F). They are omnivorous, and can be kept in a community tank with other species which do not live on or near the bottom. A layer of floating plants will provide them with the dim light they prefer.

The tiger loach *(Botia hymenophysa)* is widely distributed in south-east Asia. In a large tank it may reach a length of 25 cm (9¾ in), but this takes a long time as growth is slow. This is an aggressive fish which can only be kept with other robust species. Aquarists may be interested in setting up a special tank for loaches. This can be made to appear like a section of river bed and the water need not be deep. It can be decorated with roots, remembering that in nature the water always washes away the substrate beneath roots, leaving ideal hiding-places for the fishes. There can also be pieces of rock, particularly of slate, arranged to provide further shelter. It is a good idea to paint the tank walls black,

Botia hymenophysa

Botia macracantha

as this gives an impression of depth and cuts down reflection. The water should be kept at a temperature of 24–28°C (75–82°F), and a proportion of it should be renewed every three to four weeks.

Another popular species of about the same size is the clown loach *(Botia macracantha)*, but it is rather expensive. This is a slow-growing fish and not very robust. It requires soft water (up to 12° DH) with frequent renewal of a proportion, and fairly dim lighting. If there is plenty of shelter the fish will even come out during the day. Clown loaches are very peaceful towards one another.

There are other attractive loaches in the genus *Botia* which are quite interesting to keep in the aquarium, even though they are mainly active only during twilight. One of these is *B. horae*, which reaches a length of 10 cm (3¾ in), but usually remains smaller in captivity. This is a peaceful species, which should have soft to medium-hard water and a temperature near the bottom not exceeding 26°C (79°F). *B. lucasbahi*

Botia horae

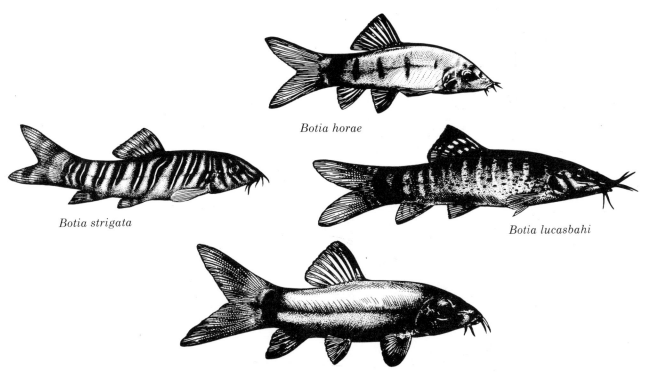

Botia horae

Botia strigata

Botia lucasbahi

Botia modesta

Acanthopsis choirorhynchus

Botia sidthimunki

is about the same size and has similar requirements. It has an elongated body and the ground coloration is ochre-brown, the dorsal fin having reddish markings near the tip. *B. modesta* resembles the preceding species in behaviour, size and requirements. It has a greyish ground colour, but this can change, according to the fish's mood, to bluish or greenish tones. The dorsal fin is yellow, but the other five are transparent. *B. striata* grows to a length of 12 cm (4¾ in), and has a particularly well-defined pattern, consisting of a deep black background crossed by golden-yellow bands which become broader towards the belly. Between these there are similarly coloured fine lines. The fins are transparent with a yellowish tinge and a pattern of black dots. This species is especially suitable for a special loach tank as it is active during the daytime.

B. sidthimunki is one of the dwarfs of the group, reaching a length of 4 cm (1½ in) at the most. The female is stouter than the male, with a more convex belly (see photograph). The pattern on the body varies between individuals. These fishes, which are active during the day, thrive best in a tank that is not too large (about 60 cm or 13 in long), and preferably without other species. They can, however, be kept in a large community tank, provided the other fishes live in the upper water layers. They will eat almost any food suitable for their size. The tank water should be soft to medium-hard, and kept at a temperature of 24–28°C (75–82°F). A proportion of the water should be renewed at frequent intervals.

Finally, there is *Acanthopsis choirorhynchus*, a large species from south-east Asia, which grows relatively slowly to a length of 18 cm (7 in). It is active at night, and it digs vigorously in the substrate, occasionally bringing up plants that are too small or insufficiently rooted, so care must be taken when setting up the tank. The water should be soft and the temperature must not exceed 26°C (79°F).

The various catfish families

Catfishes form an enormous group distributed throughout the world, except in the colder regions. They all have barbels which may be unbranched or feathery. There are over 2,000 different species, classified in about twenty families, and many of them are much too large for the home aquarium. It is therefore best to find out the size of the fishes when fully grown before making a purchase. Fishes that have grown too large do not look good in an aquarium and they may destroy the tank furnishings with a single stroke of the tail.

Most catfishes are active at night, remaining hidden by day and emerging to search for food at twilight, or when the aquarium lights are switched off. Most aquarists, however, will want to see and enjoy their fishes. This is why the armoured catfishes are so popular, for they are not so retiring during the day as the majority of their relatives. They are also a suitable size for the aquarium, being only a few centimetres long (2–4 in). Many catfishes can be kept with other species in a community tank, but some

such as members of the genus *Clarias* grow too large and become predatory. They should be kept in a tank on their own.

Catfishes of the family Mochocidae come exclusively from the tropical parts of Africa. They are nocturnal shoaling fishes which retire to a sheltered spot during the day and wait until the approach of darkness. One of the most beautiful members of this family is *Synodontis angelicus* which, like its relative *S. flavitaeniatus*, comes from tropical West Africa. When young (length 5–10 cm or 2–4 in), both species have a particularly striking coloration, but this is unfortunately lost with age; they reach a length of 20 cm (7¾ in). The upside-down catfish *(S. nigriventris)* is one of the dwarfs of the family, growing only to a length of about 6 cm (2¼ in). These catfishes are omnivorous and prefer soft water, although they will tolerate medium-hard water. The temperature should be 23–27°C (73–81°F). The females can be distinguished from the males by their greater girth. Under favourable conditions they have been bred in the aquarium. The upside-

top: *Synodontis angelicus*
above: *Synodontis flavitaeniatus*

Pimelodus clarias

Synodontis nigriventris

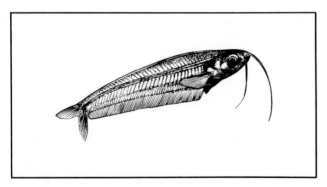

Kryptopterus bicirrhis

down catfish is so called because it has the habit of swimming upside down when grazing on the undersides of leaves, and its coloration is reversed, the belly being darker than the back.

The glass catfish *(Kryptopterus bicirrhis)*, which reaches a length of 10 cm ($3\frac{3}{4}$ in), belongs to the family Siluridae, a group sometimes known as the true catfishes. The body is very transparent. Glass catfishes, which come from Thailand, Malaysia and the Greater Sunda Islands, are active and their tank should not be too small. They are not really bottom-living fishes, but like to lurk in among plants with feathery leaves, and they must always be kept in a small group as single specimens usually die. The water should be soft to medium-hard and the temperature about 24°C (75°F). They can be fed mainly on live food, for only exceptionally will they take dried food. Nothing is known about their reproductive habits. This is not a suitable fish for the beginner.

Mystus vittatus belongs to the family Bagridae and comes from south-east Asia. Even in the aquarium this species may reach a length of 20 cm (7¾ in) and it is really only suitable for the home aquarium when quite young. The barbels are particularly long. These are mainly nocturnal fishes which remain hidden during the day. A large specimen may eat other inhabitants of the tank during the night when they are asleep. This species is not known to have bred in the aquarium.

Catfishes of the family Pimelodontidae come from central and northern South America, with a few from Central America and the Caribbean area. They have three pairs of barbels which serve as sensory organs. The family includes the genera *Microglanis, Pimelodus, Pimelodella, Pseudopimelodus, Rhamdia* and *Sorubim*. The latter grows to a large size, and is only suitable for the home aquarium when young.

A more suitable species for the average tank is *Pimelodus clarias*, which grows to a length of 30 cm (11¾ in) in the wild, but will normally be smaller in an aquarium tank. It is very easy to keep in soft water that has been made slightly acid by filtering through peat. The temperature should be 20–26°C (68–79°F).

These catfishes should be kept in a tank that is not too small (minimum length 80 cm or 30 in), with a soft, dark substrate, a few rocks and roots that are not too pale and some floating plants at the surface. These are nocturnal and twilight fishes that prefer live food, such as mosquito larvae and *Tubifex*, and they do not take readily to dead food. The members of this family have very long antenna-like barbels, and the bases of these structures are extremely sensitive to injury. It is therefore advisable when catching

Mystus vittatus

Bunocephalus kneri

these fishes to use a glass container, rather than a net. They can usually be caught quite easily in this way.

The family Bunocephalidae contains small to medium-sized catfishes, all from South America. They have been likened in appearance to a frying-pan, the head and body forming the pan and the long thin tail the handle. Although they appear to be heavily armoured they do not, in fact, have any bony plates, but only numerous large tubercles on the skin surface. They are nocturnal and spend the day in a dark hiding-place, coming out at night to search for food, when they usually swim close above the bottom.

The two species most often kept in the aquarium are *Bunocephalus bicolor* and *B. kneri*. The first species may reach a length of 15 cm (6 in), the second a little less. The water temperature at the bottom should be 20–25°C (68–77°F). When keeping catfishes it is a good idea to place the aquarium thermometer on or just above the substrate, rather than close to the water surface. These are omnivorous fishes which usually eat up the remains of food left by the other inhabitants of the tank. They like to burrow in the uppermost layer of the substrate, so when setting up the tank care should be taken to use a fine sand.

The armoured catfishes of the family Callichthyidae have a true armour in the form of bony plates which are arranged in two longitudinal rows. These plates overlap like the tiles on a roof. The rays of the pectoral, dorsal and adipose fins are spiny. Armoured catfishes should always be kept in a small shoal, never as solitary individuals. Their size is ideal for the home aquarium, most of the species in the genus *Corydoras*, for instance, being only 5–10 cm (2–4 in) long, and they are also excellent scavengers. Some of them will even breed in the aquarium. For this the breeding tank should be about 60 cm (23 in) long, with a few groups of plants and a substrate of fine sand. Females ready to spawn can be recognized by their girth. Two or three males can be put in with a single ripe female, until one can observe which fishes make a compatible pair. The remaining males must then be removed. The temperature should be raised to 26°C (79°F). Spawning can be stimulated by frequently renewing a proportion of the water. After spawning the parent fishes must be put back into their original tank to prevent them eating the eggs. The newly hatched young can be reared on very fine live food and also on dried food.

The bronze corydoras *(Corydoras aeneus)*, which grows to 7 cm (2¾ in) long, can be taken as characteristic of the genus, as regards behaviour and aquarium requirements. The body is squat, the dorsal profile much curved, the barbels short, and the dorsal fin often quite tall. This genus contains a large number of species and many of them have been bred in the aquarium.

Corydoras aeneus

Attempts at breeding are best made during the winter months (from the end of October). Naturally the armoured catfishes must be provided with hiding-places in the tank but they make less use of them, particularly during the day, than the other catfishes.

Armoured catfishes normally spend their time close to the bottom, but from time to time they can be seen to rise rapidly to the surface and gulp air. This air passes along the alimentary canal to the hindgut where its contained oxygen is absorbed by the blood vessels. This accessory method of respiration enables the fishes to survive in waters that are deficient in oxygen. Armoured catfishes will eat almost anything, and although they prefer live food they are very useful to the aquarist, for they remove scraps of food left by other fishes. They like a temperature around 24°C (75°F), and the water should be soft.

The arched corydoras *(C. arcuatus)* comes from the area of Lago Tefé on the middle Amazon. It grows to a length of 5 cm (2 in) and is characterized by the very tall and pointed dorsal fin and by the curved longitudinal stripe running along each side from the mouth to the caudal peduncle. The leopard corydoras *(C. julii)*, from tributaries of the Amazon, grows up to 6 cm ($2\frac{1}{4}$ in) long. With a pattern consisting of rows of fine dots, it is not easily confused with other species. It differs, for example, from the black-spotted corydoras *(C. melanistius)* in lacking the dark band running through the eye. In *C. melanistius* the dark pattern of the dorsal fin extends onto the body and the arrangement of the black spots is not so reminiscent of a pearl necklace as

Corydoras punctatus

Corydoras melanistius

Corydoras arcuatus

Corydoras julii

Corydoras myersi

Corydoras hastatus

Corydoras schwartzi

it is in the leopard corydoras. Myers' corydoras *(C. myersi)* comes from the Amazon west of Manaus, and it also grows to 6 cm ($2\frac{1}{4}$ in). At first sight it appears to have the same dorsal longitudinal band as the arched corydoras, but in fact this extends forwards only to the top of the forehead. Schwartz's corydoras *(C. schwartzi)* is another spotted species, but with a pattern that is much coarser than in the two spotted species previously mentioned, and its spots are arranged more irregularly. *C. vermelinhos* is an active member of the family which likes a sunlit tank with a soft, sandy substrate. This is an omnivorous species which should be kept in a shoal; it often lives for quite a time in the aquarium. There are also two particularly small species, *C. hastatus* and *C. pygmaeus*, both of which only grow to a length of 3–4 cm (up to $1\frac{1}{2}$ in), and a really tiny fish, *C. cochui*, which only reaches about 2.5 cm (1 in) in length; unfortunately the latter is only rarely seen in the home aquarium.

The family Loricariidae includes the genera *Farlowella*, *Loricaria*, *Otocinclus*, *Plecostomus* and *Xenocara*, all from South America. These have the head and body protected by bony plates that overlap like roof tiles. *Loricaria filamentosa* comes from the area of the Rio Magdalena in Colombia. In the wild or in a very large tank it may reach a length of 20 cm ($7\frac{3}{4}$ in), of which almost half is tail. In most aquarium tanks, where the conditions are not absolutely ideal, it remains much smaller.

These catfishes can be bred in captivity. At the approach of the spawning period the sexually mature male acquires a number of bristles on the sides of the head. The female, on the other hand, becomes stouter than the male. Spawning takes place after vigorous and prolonged cleaning of dark rocks on the bottom. The eggs are white when laid, but before hatching they become pale brown. If the temperature on the bottom is 23–24°C (73–75°F) the eggs should hatch in eight to ten days. The male frees the fry from the eggcases by striking them with his fins. The young fishes can then be transferred to a tank without substrate (otherwise they are scarcely discernible), and after they have consumed their yolk sac they start to feed immediately. They are not fastidious and will take almost anything that will enter their mouth. It should not be forgotten

Loricaria filamentosa

Loricaria filamentosa, head showing appendages

that these catfishes require a certain amount of plant food.

In the wild, the loricariid catfishes live on the bottom where they search rocks, roots and the substrate for food. The mouth is suctorial with thick, broad lips: a useful adaptation for life in the often fast-flowing rivers of their home range. These fishes are well protected against attack by their tough armour. They apparently have the ability to wink, but this is not really so. Unlike all other fishes they have a structure known as the iris lobe, which projects down across the pupil. This lobe helps to regulate the amount of light falling on the eye during daylight hours, but in darkness it contracts so that the pupil is no longer partially obscured.

Loricariid catfishes are efficient consumers of algae, but they do not damage higher plants. At a temperature on the bottom of 20–25°C (68–77°F) they will live for some years. The tank water should be soft, or at any rate not harder than medium-hard. During the day the fishes show themselves on the bottom or on pieces of rock, for they do not always hide away. They can be fed on a variety of foods. Other members of the family Loricariidae that can be kept in the aquarium include *Otocinclus affinis* and *O. vittatus*, which do not exceed 4–6 cm ($1\frac{1}{2}$–$2\frac{1}{4}$ in) in length.

Brachygobius xanthozona

retreat rapidly when threatened. They should on no account be put into soft water, but should be given hard water to which some sea salt or sea water has been added. The tank can be provided with rocks, and it does not matter, of course, if these contain calcium. The water should be kept at a temperature of 24–28°C (75–82°F) and a proportion can be renewed at intervals, taking care to maintain the small content of salt. Gobies feed principally on live food, and do not willingly take dried food.

The goby family

Gobies are mostly marine, but a few live in fresh or brackish waters. The best known of these is the bumblebee fish *(Brachygobius xanthozona)*, a mainly brackish-water species from Java, Sumatra and Borneo which also occurs in fresh waters. It grows up to only 5 cm (2 in) in length.

Bumblebee fishes are best kept in a tank on their own (a species tank). They live mainly in the vicinity of their hiding-places, to which they

Spiny eels

Spiny eels of the family Mastacembelidae come from waters in Africa and south-east Asia that are rich in vegetation. They are nocturnal fishes that feed mainly on various kinds of worms. Most spiny eels live in coastal areas where the fresh water is mixed with a small amount of salt. In the aquarium, therefore, it is best to add about 2 teaspoonfuls of salt to every 10 litres ($2\frac{1}{4}$ gallons) of tank water.

Macrognathus aculeatus, from south-east Asia, grows to a length of 35 cm ($13\frac{3}{4}$ in). Its tank should have a soft, sandy or muddy bottom, with rock, a few plants and perhaps a short length of piping to provide cover. These fishes start to become active towards evening. They must be given a varied diet. The upper part of the body is chocolate-brown, the belly pale, and the dorsal fin has a row of peacock-eye markings. These fishes can be aggressive, and will even bite a hand if it comes too near. In general, they can

Macrognathus aculeatus

Mastacembelus armatus

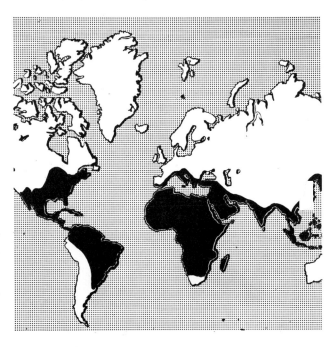

Distribution of toothcarps

scarcely be regarded as suitable fishes for the beginner.

Mastacembelus armatus, also from south-east Asia, is a giant, which under certain conditions can reach a length of up to 80 cm (31 in), and its appetite matches its size. It must, of course, only be kept with fishes of its own size, as it will devour anything smaller.

The toothcarp families

Toothcarps are widely distributed in certain parts of America, Africa, southern Europe and Asia, but not in Australia. They are classified in two main families: the egg-laying toothcarps (Cyprinodontidae) and the livebearing toothcarps (Poeciliidae). The latter come originally only from the New World, the former from America, Africa, Asia and southern Europe.

101

Egg-laying toothcarps

The majority of the egg-laying toothcarps or killifishes come from tropical regions and small species predominate. They should only be kept by experienced aquarists, and preferably in species tanks (i.e. without other species). The family contains approximately 500 species, and new ones are still being discovered.

The species of *Aphyosemion* come from tropical West Africa, where they live in streams, ditches and ponds. Some of the species in the original genus *Aphyosemion* are now classified in a separate genus, *Roloffia*. Further to the east, throughout much of Central Africa, there are species of the genus *Aplocheilichthys*. Other West African toothcarps include the species of *Epiplatys*, and from East and Central Africa and Madagascar come representatives of the genera *Nothobranchius* and *Pachypanchax*. Many of the latter live in waters which dry up at certain times, and the adult fishes die. In fact these seasonal fishes spend part of their life cycle as eggs buried in the mud. As soon as the pond fills up with water after the dry season the eggs hatch and the life cycle starts afresh. These fishes require extremely soft water if they are to thrive, and particularly if they are to breed. Similar conditions are found in South America where the genera represented include *Austrofundulus*, *Cynolebias*, *Cynopoecilus*, *Pterolebias* and *Rachovia*.

Northern and Central America have the genera *Chriopeops*, *Cubanichthys*, *Cyprinodon*, *Fundulus*, *Jordanella* and *Rivulus*. Here, too, some species live as seasonal fishes, as for example the desert pupfish *(Cyprinodon macularius)*, which comes from parts of Arizona, Lower California and northern Sonora in Mexico.

From the Mediterranean Sea and extending eastwards to Iran there are species of the genus *Aphanius*. These require slightly brackish water.

Finally, there are the genera *Aplocheilus* and *Oryzias* from the tropical and subtropical areas of Asia, from India to Japan. *Oryzias* is now placed in its own family, the Oryziatidae. Species of *Aplocheilus* live at the water surface and some are very predatory, even when young. In spite of this they are popular aquarium fishes, for they are beautifully coloured and they breed readily.

Provided the conditions are correct, it is very simple to breed egg-laying toothcarps. Most of them require soft, acid water, while some do better with a pH around 7. They do not, however, tolerate changes of water involving any large proportion of the total. Some of the species lay their eggs and attach them to plants or tufts of algae. Others spawn on the bottom and there are two groups: those that lay on the surface of the substrate, and those that lay eggs actually in the substrate. The majority lay on the surface, but the South American species in the genera *Austrofundulus*, *Cynolebias* and *Pterolebias* burrow into the substrate to spawn. The period between egg-laying and hatching may be a few

Reproductive behaviour in toothcarps:
left: spawning on the substrate *(Epiplatys)*
centre: spawning in the substrate *(Pterolebias)*
right: mating in livebearers

Aplocheilus lineatus, male above, female below

Aplocheilus panchax

weeks, or it may be several months. In extreme cases the eggs may not hatch for several years. This is important, for it allows for the survival of the species over long periods of drought.

Aplocheilus lineatus from India and Ceylon (Sri Lanka) reaches a length of 10 cm (3¾ in). This is a hardy surface-living fish which occurs in various colour forms. The blue panchax *(Aplocheilus panchax)* also lives at the surface and it has a more eastern distribution, extending from Bangladesh to the Greater Sunda Islands. It is also a hardy fish, reaching a length of up to 8 cm (3 in), and again there are several different colour varieties, depending upon the place of origin.

These two species require tanks with a maximum surface area, so a wide flat aquarium is recommended. The vegetation in the lower water layers is of no consequence to the fishes so it can be made to suit the aquarist's aesthetic sense. On the other hand, the plants growing in the upper water layers are important to the fishes, which prefer to have plants with leaves that float at the surface. Free-floating plants such as *Riccia* are also suitable, but need culling when they grow into luxuriant mats. The water should be mature (i.e. not straight from the tap) and not hard. Filtration through peat is an advantage, particularly if breeding is to be attempted.

These fishes are good jumpers so their tanks should be well covered. In spite of their predatory tendencies they can be kept together with other species, but care should be taken to ensure that there are no smaller or younger fishes in the tank. *Aplocheilus* species feed on all kinds of live food, such as *Tubifex*, mosquito larvae, water-fleas, *Cyclops* and flies, and they will also take dried food.

Other related species are the green panchax *(A. blockii)* which only grows to 5 cm (2 in), the Ceylon killifish *(A. dayi)* and the form sold on the market as *A. 'siamensis'*. These fishes all live at the surface, although *A. blockii* occasionally swims in the middle water layers. They should be kept in the same way as *A. lineatus* and *A. panchax*.

The best-known egg-laying toothcarps, namely species of the genus *Aphyosemion*, come from the African continent. These are very beautiful

below: *Aphyosemion australe 'hjerresenii'*, male
bottom: *Aphyosemion gardneri,* male

Aphyosemion sjoestedti

Aphyosemion australe australe, males above and below, female in centre

fishes but they are not all easy to keep. With a few exceptions they do not exceed 6 cm ($2\frac{1}{4}$ in) in length. As every aquarist knows, the most handsome species often raise the most problems. For instance, these fishes only live a short time. They occur in small streams, ditches and ponds in tropical West Africa, which dry up during the hot season, killing the fishes, but leaving their eggs viable. In the short period between the onset of the rainy season and the next dry season, the fish have to hatch from the eggs, grow to sexual maturity, pair up and produce the next batch of eggs.

The lyretail *(Aphyosemion australe)* is one of the most commonly kept species in the genus. There is also an orange-red form known as *A. australe 'hjerresenii'.* The lyretail comes from the Ogooue delta near Cape Lopez in Gabon, West Africa. It grows to a length of 6 cm ($2\frac{1}{4}$ in), and should be kept at a temperature around 22°C (72°F). Another attractive fish is *A. gardneri* which grows to 5 cm (2 in) and comes from equatorial West Africa. The fish now known as *A. sjoestedti* was previously called *A. gulare coeruleum*, and the former *A. sjoestedti* is now placed in the genus *Roloffia* and known as *R. occidentalis.* Other species sometimes available are *A. bivittatum*, which has a number of subspecies, the rarely kept *A. arnoldi*, the red *A. cognatum*, *A. fallax* and *A. vexillifer.*

Although some of these species can be kept together, the specialist in this group normally keeps them in separate species tanks, and this allows them to show their full beauty. The tanks should have a length of about 20–40 cm (8–16 in). The water should be soft and acid and at a temperature of about 22°C (72°F). Vegetation is really unnecessary, but there can be small groups of low-growing plants. These fishes feed mainly on live food, but will also take some dried food.

Species of the genus *Epiplatys* mostly come from areas along the coasts of West Africa, where they live in standing or slow-flowing waters. These are typical surface-living fishes with a straight dorsal profile and a mouth that

Epiplatys annulatus

104

faces upwards. They require a tank with a large surface area and a layer of floating plants with varying leaf shapes. They can be kept in a community tank, and this has the advantage that the other species will eat any food that falls down from the surface. The sexes are easy to distinguish, the males being larger than the females and more brightly coloured. The water temperature should be 26–28°C (79–82°F). The species of *Epiplatys* lay eggs attached to plants. They have an interesting courtship. The male drives the female very hard, and at intervals presents his most brilliant coloration. Sometimes he presses the female on to the spawning substrate. The eggs hatch some seven to twenty-eight days after they are laid.

and may live for up to three years when well cared for. The colours intensify during courtship, the fins of the male showing very beautiful tones of red. The female lacks these colours and is always somewhat paler. The water should be soft (4–8° DH), slightly acid, and kept at a temperature of 24°C (75°F). The tank itself can be quite small, a length of 30–40 cm (12–16 in) being quite sufficient. These are not suitable fishes for the beginner, but in experienced hands they can be bred.

The genus *Nothobranchius* is centred on the coastal areas of East Africa. The species are again seasonal fishes, and even more short-lived than members of the genus *Aphyosemion*. The three best-known species of *Nothobranchius* differ from each other quite markedly and so they are not difficult to distinguish. These are *Nothobranchius orthonotus, N. palmqvisti* and *N. rachovii*. The latter grows to 5 cm (2 in), the others slightly larger. These forms are not all treated in the same way. They should, of course, be kept in separate species tanks. *N. orthonotus* and *N. palmqvisti* require water with a hardness of 6–10° DH and slightly acid (pH 6.8), at a normal temperature of 22–24°C (72–75°F). For breeding the temperature should be raised by a few degrees. *N. rachovii* is rather more demanding, for it should be kept in very soft water (2–5° DH) with an acid reaction (pH 6.5), and at a temperature around 24°C (75°F). Equipment for measuring the pH can now be bought quite inexpensively.

Epiplatys longiventralis

The firemouth epiplatys *(Epiplatys dageti,* formerly *E. chaperi)* comes from West Africa (Sierra Leone to Ghana) and is suitable for a community tank; it grows to 6 cm ($2\frac{1}{4}$ in). This is an omnivorous species which will attack young fishes. It is easily confused with *E. longiventralis* which comes from the same region, and also grows to the same length. The rocket panchax *(E. annulatus)*, from the region between Guinea and Liberia, grows to about 4 cm ($1\frac{1}{2}$ in) in length,

Nothobranchius spp.

Nothobranchius rachovii

The species of *Nothobranchius* spawn on the bottom. They can be kept and bred in quite small tanks, except in the case of *N. rachovii* which requires rather more space. There is no need to have any plants. The substrate should consist of a layer (not too thick) of peat fragments, which has several advantages. It is dark, it keeps the water acid, and it provides the fishes with the correct conditions for spawning.

In the wild, the *Nothobranchius* species feed on insects and their larvae, so their diet in the aquarium should include some of these. In fact,

Cyprinodon macularius, female above, male below

be a layer of peat about 4 cm (1½ in) thick, and any vegetation round the edges must leave sufficient space in the centre of the tank for swimming. The males are considerably larger than the females and rather aggressive, so care should be taken even when these fishes are kept in a separate tank without other species. A few pieces of root fixed into position will serve to define the limits of individual territories. The water must be soft, the hardness not exceeding 10° DH but preferably lower, and at a temperature of about 22°C (72°F). The pH should be around 6.5. *Pterolebias* feeds on insects and will greedily devour any freshly caught flies, and of course in the aquarium any form of live food, but they do not normally take much dried food.

they will also take other live food, such as *Tubifex*, water-fleas, *Cyclops* and young fishes, for instance newly born guppies, but they do not care for dried food.

The few species of *Cyprinodon* are restricted to the desert region in the south-west of the United States. They are not particularly beautiful, apart from the male of *C. macularius* which shows brilliant steel-blue coloration. The desert pupfish *(C. macularius)* reaches a length of up to 4.5 cm (1¾ in). It requires hard water (15–25° DH), with some added salt. The tank need not be very large, in fact one with a length of 20 cm (7¾ in) would suffice for four to eight specimens. There should be two to three times as many females as males, and there must be some shelter for the former, as the males will chase them around vigorously. Some dense vegetation will also help, and it makes the tank more attractive. The water temperature should be 25–27°C (77–81°F), and the diet should consist mainly of live food, which these fishes prefer to dried food.

The species of *Pterolebias* come from South America and their males have conspicuous, brightly coloured caudal and anal fins. Like the species of *Cynolebias*, these fishes lay their eggs not on the surface of the peat, but buried in the substrate. *Pterolebias peruensis* from Peru is a fast-swimming species which grows to a length of about 8 cm (3 in). The tank should, therefore, be reasonably large, and a length of 60–80 cm (24–30 in) is recommended. The substrate should

Typical habitat of *Cyprinodon macularius*, Saratoga Springs, USA

The genus *Roloffia* is still not very well known. Some of the more beautiful species are *R. bertholdi*, *R. geryi*, *R. occidentalis*, *R. roloffi* and *R. toddi*. These fishes from tropical West Africa all spawn on the bottom, and in general their habits are like those of the *Aphyosemion* species. The red aphyosemion *Roloffia occidentalis* grows to a length of 9 cm (3½ in) and occurs in West Africa (Sierra Leone). The tank for this species should

Xiphophorus helleri, an attractive hybrid form

Xiphophorus helleri, Simpson high-fin form

be at least 30 cm (12 in) long, with a few plants and pieces of root arranged to divide up the area. The males tend to be aggressive towards one another. The water should have a hardness not exceeding 10° DH, and should be filtered through peat and kept at a temperature of 20–24°C (68–75°F). These fishes can be fed on mosquito larvae, *Tubifex*, water-fleas, *Cyclops*, whiteworms (not too many), small earthworms and freshly caught houseflies.

Livebearing toothcarps

Swordtails, guppies and platies are among the best-known and most interesting aquarium fishes, particularly for the beginner. Not only do they produce live young, they are also highly adaptable fishes. They form the family Poeciliidae and all the species come from the New World, their range extending from southern USA through Central America, including the Caribbean Islands, to northern Argentina. They live in quiet stretches of water with dense vegetation. In the aquarium they should be given water that is not too soft, but which has stood for some time. Certain species which come from estuarine regions need the addition of a little sea salt.

In this family the sexes are easy to distinguish. The males have such characters as a brilliantly coloured caudal fin (*Poecilia reticulata*), a very tall dorsal fin (*P. latipinna* and *P. velifera*) or a caudal fin elongated to form a 'sword' *(Xiphophorus helleri)*. All males have a quite characteristic copulatory organ known as gonopodium, which can be seen below the body. The male uses the gonopodium to introduce sperm into the body of the female, and she is able to store the sperm and so continue to produce live young for a long time after mating with a male.

The phenomenon of sex reversal occurs in some of the livebearers. For instance, a completely adult and sexually mature female swordtail, which has already produced several broods of young, can change into a male that is capable of breeding as such. The change takes several weeks. The anal fin of the female becomes modified to form a gonopodium, while the lower rays of the caudal fin grow into a 'sword', the characteristic feature of the male swordtail.

Xiphophorus helleri, lyretail form

In various species the males have gonopodia of the same or similar structure and are able to mate with females of more than one species. This happens quite frequently in the aquarium, and hybrid livebearers are very commonly produced by accident. In addition there are of course certain aquarists who indulge in hybridization with a view to producing new forms. Such breeding experiments have produced fancy fishes such as the wagtail guppy and many others. The production of strains with elongated and enlarged fins is a particularly popular pursuit in certain aquarium circles. Thus there is the Simpson swordtail with its flag-like dorsal fin, the various lyretail forms of molly and, in particular, the enormous variety of dorsal and caudal fin shapes in the guppy. This most famous of all aquarium

Poecilia velifera, an albino form with lyretail

fishes was first described scientifically in 1859 as *Poecilia reticulata*. Its popular name is in honour of the Reverend Robert J. L. Guppy, a parson who brought living specimens from Trinidad to the British Museum (Natural History) in London.

The livebearing toothcarps play an important part in the aquarium world, although the number of genera and species is not very large. Many of those sold on the market are genetically very mixed.

The mollies, now classified in the genus *Poecilia*, but formerly as *Mollienesia*, include the sailfin mollies *Poecilia velifera* and *P. latipinna*, as well as the pointed-mouth molly (*P. sphenops*).

These fishes have a distribution range extending from the southern United States to Yucatan in Mexico, and they occur mainly in brackish estuaries. Their maximum length is 12 cm (4¾ in), but in the aquarium they only reach about three-quarters of this length. They like plenty of warmth, and a temperature of about 26°C (79°F) or somewhat higher is usually recommended. They are not very aggressive, so they can be kept together with other livebearers. Mollies require a well-lit aquarium tank that is not too small, but with plenty of vegetation. They are not in any way demanding as regards water quality, but the addition of a small amount of salt is beneficial. The selected or hybrid mollies with enlarged fins should be given plenty of space for swimming, otherwise the wonderful fins of the males will not attain their full development.

The platy (*Xiphophorus maculatus*) and its relative the variatus platy (*Xiphophorus variatus*) are also widespread in the home aquarium, and they interbreed very frequently, the gonopodia of the males being similar in structure. In fact the hybridization of these two species has, over the years, produced an enormous number of genetically mixed aquarium fishes. The original species come from Central America and grow to about 10 cm (3¾ in) in length, but they are smaller than this in the aquarium. Platies and variatus are extremely easy to keep. They have a good appetite and will eat mosquito larvae and other

Xiphophorus maculatus

Xiphophorus helleri, a red selected form

Xiphophorus helleri, an attractive hybrid form

small live food, as well as dried food, and they also like a certain amount of plant food.

Swordtails *(Xiphophorus helleri)* are really ideal fishes for the average aquarist, for they have brilliant coloration (mainly red) and an attractive 'sword' in the male. They are undemanding and will live in any kind of water, except very soft, and will eat almost anything. In addition, they live for a long time and are very prolific. They grow to a length of up to 12 cm (4¾ in), but the male is smaller if the 'sword' is excluded, and they come originally from Central America (Mexico and Guatemala). Nowadays it is doubtful whether many aquarium swordtails are truly wild caught, but large numbers are in hatcheries, for instance in Florida. Several new selected swordtail varieties have been produced in recent years.

Swordtails are ideal in a community tank for they are normally peaceful towards other fishes and towards other members of their own species. Occasionally the males may fight each other. Their permanent tank should not be too small, and in any case not less than 60 cm (24 in) in length. It should have dense marginal vegetation and space in the centre for swimming, with a few rocks and roots. Swordtails thrive best in medium-hard water at a temperature of 22–25°C (72–77°F), but they are not damaged if this occasionally drops a few degrees for a short period.

Xiphophorus helleri, long-finned hybrids with lyre tails

The number of young in a brood depends upon the size of the female, so young specimens are not ideal for breeding. Large females often produce 160 or more live young at a time. In most cases it is only necessary to have one active male to mate with a number of females. It should also be remembered that a mated female can store sperms and so produce several broods from a single mating. If a brood happens to be born in a community tank, care should be taken to ensure that there are sufficient hiding-places (feathery-leaved plants and certain species of

Cryptocoryne) for the young fishes. Livebearers are often kept together with angelfishes, and if this is the case few of the young from a brood will survive, as the cichlids find them an attractive form of live food.

Much has been written about the guppy *(Poecilia reticulata)*, which comes originally from northern South America, Barbados and Trinidad. Numerous crosses have been carried

above: *Poecilia reticulata*, male with triangle tail

Poecilia reticulata, four varieties with fantastic patterns

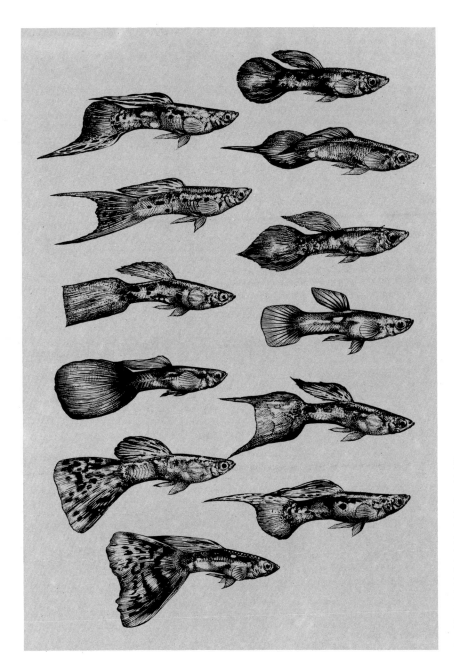

Standard forms of guppy:
Left vertical row, from above:
bottom sword
double sword
flagtail
veiltail
fantail
triangle
Right vertical row, from above:
round tail
pintail
speartail
spadetail
lyretail
top sword

out and the results are very different from the original wild stock. Guppy societies in many parts of the world have encouraged hybridization and selection and have drawn up rules for judging the finer points in guppydom, just as other societies are devoted to the breeding and selection of domestic races of cats and dogs.

The maintenance of guppies in a community tank raises no problems at all, as they have no special requirements. The sexes can be distinguished at a relatively early age: the males are smaller, more slender and they grow brightly coloured fins as soon as they start to become sexually mature. The females, on the other hand, have a considerably greater girth and they grow to almost twice the length of the males. Their coloration is a uniform grey with occasional blue or green iridescence on the scales. The tank

113

Dermogenys siamensis

for guppies should have dense marginal vegetation. If they are kept with angelfishes or other voracious forms, such as barbs, their young should be given some protection. Guppies are not very sensitive to changes in the quality of the water, but soft water should be avoided. They prefer a temperature of about 23°C (73°F), but no harm is done if this occasionally drops to 18°C (64°F). They will eat all kinds of live food, as well as lettuce, algae, boiled spinach, finely sieved oatmeal, and deep-frozen and dried foods.

Finally, there are a few livebearing fishes which do not belong among the livebearing toothcarps (Poeciliidae). These include the half-beaks of the family Hemirhamphidae, so-called from the short upper mandible and the elongated, immobile lower mandible. The best known of these is the common half-beak *Dermogenys pusillus* which was first imported into Europe about 1905. Other species are *D. pogonognathus*, *D. sumatranus* and *D. siamensis*, the latter being shown above. These all live at the surface, and the peculiar mouth is well adapted for picking up insects from the surface of the water. In the aquarium they can be given mosquitoes and

their larvae, fruitflies, water-fleas, *Cyclops* and *Tubifex*, and will also take some fine dried food and freeze-dried food. They will not, however, follow after sinking food and are unable to pick up anything from the bottom, so they should be fed slowly. From time to time they can be given whiteworms and freshly caught houseflies. When the tank contains pregnant females, extra care should be taken to ensure that the diet is varied and rich in vitamins. In a pregnant female the dark eyes of the embryos can be seen through the belly wall several days before the birth.

Newly purchased half-beaks should not be put into a freshly established tank, as they may become very alarmed by their new surroundings and in their panic may damage the elongated lower jaw. When this happens they usually die. It is therefore best to leave the tank without fishes for some time, but to give it plenty of light so that algae grow on at least the side and back walls. Half-beaks, which come from south-east Asia, vary in length according to species and sex. Usually the males are up to about 7 cm (2¾ in) long and the females about 2 cm (¾ in) more.

The rarely imported *D. pogonognathus (= Hemirhamphodon pogonognathus)* occasionally shows the reverse, with males about 8 cm (3 in) long and females usually 2 cm ($\frac{3}{4}$ in) shorter.

The tank for half-beaks should have a fairly large surface area, but its height is less important. Floating plants with large leaves at the surface will provide cover, and if the tank is to contain other fishes these should belong to species which live in the deeper water layers. The water should be neither too soft nor too hard, so 10–20° DH is recommended, and its temperature at the surface should be 26–30°C (79–86°F). Newly imported specimens require water containing 5–10% sea water. Pregnant females must be removed to a special tank with shallow water (15 cm or 6 in deep at the most). This can also have floating plants and the water must be of the same type as that in the main tank. The temperature in the breeding tank must not sink below 28°C (82°F) otherwise the young will suffer. In most cases the broods contain between fifteen and forty young, which can be fed on *Artemia* nauplii. Half-beaks are not really suitable fishes for the beginner.

Lepomis gibbosus

The various families of perch-like fishes

The perch-like fishes or Percomorphi form a very large group containing numerous families, some of which have representatives in the aquarium. The family Cichlidae has the greatest number of species that are suitable for the home aquarium, but before dealing with them in some detail it may be best to look at a few of the smaller families.

Sunfishes

The sunfishes or Centrarchidae all come from the eastern and central areas of North America and are cold-water species. They are kept in a well-lit tank with a substrate of fine sand, some cold-water plants and a few rocks and roots. They can also be kept in tanks or ponds out of doors, but not if the water is likely to freeze during the winter. When they have become acclimatized and are no longer young they may be damaged if they are transferred to a different type of water.

A good representative of the family is the pumpkinseed *(Lepomis gibbosus)*, with a distribution extending from the Great Lakes near the Canadian border to Texas and Florida. In the aquarium these fishes sometimes reach a length of about 14 cm ($5\frac{1}{2}$ in), but in the wild or in an outside pond they grow to about 20 cm ($7\frac{3}{4}$ in). They are omnivorous and in no way demanding.

Archerfishes

Archerfishes of the family Toxotidae are interesting to keep on account of their habit of shooting down flies. They are primarily brackish-water fishes which live in the coastal areas of India and south-east Asia, including the Sunda Islands and further east. They are capable of shooting down insects perched on branches or other objects above the water. They do this by forcefully expelling drops of water from the mouth and their aim is remarkably accurate. A skilled archerfish can shoot down a fly at a range of 150 cm (60 in). Young individuals learn rapidly and can soon spit for distances of a few inches.

Archerfishes live mainly in the mangrove zone along the coasts where there is plenty of insect life. To keep them successfully in the aquarium they must be given a large shallow tank with a maximum surface area and not too many plants. Young fishes often do well in ordinary fresh water, but older specimens become very sensitive to the quality of the water, which should contain about 3 teaspoonfuls of salt to 10 litres (2.2 gallons) of water. The surface temperature should be between 26 and 28°C (79–82°F), and it is a good idea to change a proportion of the water occasionally. Archerfishes are not omnivorous, but prefer insects of a suitable size, dropped on the surface, and will also take scraps of meat placed in the water.

Scatophagus 'rubrifrons'

Fingerfishes

Fingerfishes (family Monodactylidae) do not live primarily in fresh waters. They are really brackish-water fishes which sometimes move into pure sea water. Young specimens sold in shops or stores are usually living in fresh water, and they can be left in this until they are about 2.5 cm (1 in) long. They should then be gradually acclimatized to living in brackish water, ending up with water containing about 3 teaspoonfuls of salt to every 10 litres (2.2 gallons). If this is not done the fishes will eventually die, when they are about 5 cm (2 in) long.

Argusfishes

Argusfishes (family Scatophagidae) live in coastal areas of south-east Asia and northern Australia, and should therefore be regarded as brackish-water species. They live in shoals, often in estuaries, and can grow up to 30 cm (11¾ in) in length. As they are mainly vegetarian, a regimen requiring large amounts of food, they produce large amounts of faeces. In an aquarium tank this can lead to gross pollution, and so the installation of a filter is strongly recommended. Although originally vegetarian, they readily take any other food, and are often seen feeding in the vicinity of sewage outlets. Argusfishes have two dorsal fins and the two forms seen in the aquarium tanks are *Scatophagus argus* and *S. 'rubrifrons'*. Most authorities regard the latter as merely a variant of the former. They

should be kept in a tank at least 100 cm (40 in) long, with a few roots for decoration. The water should have a supplement of salt, as recommended for archerfishes.

Nandids

Nandids (family Nandidae) are the survivors of a group of fishes that was once widely distributed. They are found in South America, Africa and south-east Asia. Their geographical distribution in Africa and South America supports the theory of continental drift, for the surviving species live in those parts of the two continents which would have been close to each other if the theory were true, namely north-eastern South America and the large 'bend' in the western coast of Africa. They are small, predatory fishes with a very large mouth and an astonishing appetite. They can swallow prey that is three-quarters of their own length.

The badis *(Badis badis)* is a very attractively coloured fish, up to 8 cm (3 in) long, which comes from south-east Asia. It has recently been classified in a family by itself (the Badidae) and placed with the anabantoids. The coloration can change quite rapidly. Its popularity in the aquarium world is also due to the fact that it is not so voracious as the other members of the family. Nevertheless, when several are kept together in a species tank they may become aggressive towards one another, as so often happens with many of the cichlids. They can be

Badis badis

Polycentrus schomburgki

ready to pounce with lightning speed on its prey. These fishes grow to a length of 10 cm ($3\frac{3}{4}$ in) at the most, and they come from Venezuela, Guyana and the island of Trinidad. Their coloration provides camouflage when they are among vegetation, and the very protrusible mouth is excellently adapted for swallowing relatively large prey. Another member of the same family is the South American leaf-fish *(Monocirrhus polyacanthus)* which has the same general habits and the same method of feeding. It grows up to 8 cm (3 in) in length. Both these species prefer very soft, slightly acid water, and they should never be kept in a community tank, but in a separate species tank with plenty of hiding-places and subdued lighting. Their favourite diet is small fishes, but they can become accustomed to feeding on pieces of heart and liver.

Cichlids

The cichlids (family Cichlidae) form one of the main families from which aquarists have selected a large number of species. They range from the majestic angelfishes and the extremely handsome discus to the brilliantly coloured forms which have only recently started to come in from some of the East African lakes. Not all of them are as popular as the angelfishes, for many have a rather bad reputation among aquarists. They dig in the bottom, uproot the plants, bite or kill other fishes, or quite simply are aggressive, voracious predators. Naturally such inborn ten-

kept in water with a hardness of 10–15° DH, at a temperature of 26–28°C (79–82°F). The tank should be provided with several good hiding-places, otherwise the fishes will always remain rather shy. The males can be recognized by the concave belly profile, the females' being convex.

Schomburgk's leaf-fish *(Polycentrus schomburgki)* from South America is a voracious predator which generally lurks in among the plants, dencies are not lost in the aquarium environment. There are, however, many species which do not behave in this way, and if an aggressive species is introduced into a tank where it causes a tumult, this is the fault of the aquarist, not the fishes.

The cichlids can be conveniently divided into those coming originally from Asia and America, and those from Africa. There are only two Asiatic cichlids and although both have appeared on the market, the more popular of them used to be the orange chromide *Etroplus maculatus* from India and Ceylon (Sri Lanka), which grows to a length of 8–10 cm (3–3¾ in). It is not so often kept nowadays.

Pelmatochromis thomasi

Pseudotropheus elongatus

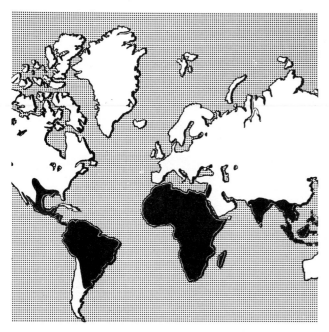

Distribution of cichlids

For many years species from South America accounted for the majority of the cichlids kept by aquarists, although it is possible that those more recently imported from Africa may soon be outstripping them. The best known of the South American cichlids belong to the genera *Aequidens*, *Apistogramma*, *Astronotus*, *Cichlasoma*, *Crenicara*, *Geophagus*, *Nannacara*, *Pterophyllum* and *Symphysodon*. In recent years

118

Tilapia mariae

ichthyologists have been revising the nomenclature of some of these fishes, but in the meantime it seems best to retain the older, established names.

Among the African cichlids, species of the genera *Haplochromis, Hemichromis, Nanochromis, Pelmatochromis, Steatocranus* and *Tilapia* have been known and kept for many years. The newly imported species from the African lakes have brought new life into what was rather a backwater of the aquarium world. These come from Lake Tanganyika and Lake Malawi (formerly Nyasa). The imports from Malawi include many species of the genera *Labeotropheus, Pseudotropheus* and *Melanochromis*. The Tanganyika cichlids, which are not so brilliantly coloured, have spread more slowly. Here, apart from the very beautiful species of *Julidochromis,*

Brood protection in cichlids:
left: substrate spawner *(Cichlasoma meeki)*, with young
centre: young discus fishes feeding on the parent's flank
right: mouthbrooder *(Tilapia)* with young retreating into
the parent's mouth

there are representatives of the genera *Tropheus, Eretmodus, Lamprologus, Limnotilapia, Limnochromis* and *Lobochilotes.*

Most cichlids are relatively easy to breed, and this is one of the reasons for their popularity. However, within this large family there is great variety in the way the young are tended. In some species both parents protect the brood, in others only the father or the mother. Then there are the mouthbrooders, which show an astonishing form of brood protection. In these species, either one of the parents, but usually the female, takes the fertilized eggs into its mouth and incubates them there until they hatch. Subsequently the mouth continues to provide shelter for the young for a further period. On the approach of danger the young swimming around the parent fish will turn and swim back into the mouth. Much has been written on the way in which the discus fishes rear their young. In these species the eggs are laid on the bottom, and shortly after hatching the fry attach themselves to the parents' flanks, where for several days they live on a skin secretion, which they literally 'graze' from their parents.

The cichlids are all territorial, so it is often difficult to keep several males of a species in a relatively small tank, because they fight one

another very vigorously when they are sexually mature. It is therefore essential to find out as much as possible about a given species before starting to keep it.

One of the best known of the South American cichlids is the blue acara *(Aequidens pulcher,* formerly *A. latifrons)* which comes from Colombia and Panama and grows to a length of up to 15 cm (6 in). This is one of the most peaceful of the cichlids, and it does not require a very large tank (minimum length 60–80 cm or 24–32 in). There should be plenty of shelter, including some plants with large leaves. The tank water, at a temperature of about 24°C (75°F), should not be too hard and a third of it should be renewed at fairly frequent intervals, say three to four weeks. Blue acaras will eat almost any foods offered whether live, dried, deep-frozen or freeze-dried.

It is difficult to distinguish the sexes in *A. pulcher.* When the spawning period approaches they should be separated from any smaller fishes in the tank, as their territorial activities cause a great amount of commotion. They usually spawn on rocks, rarely on plants, and both sexes take part in tending the newly hatched young fishes. Under favourable conditions a good pair may be ready to breed again a few weeks later. If this

Apistogramma agassizi

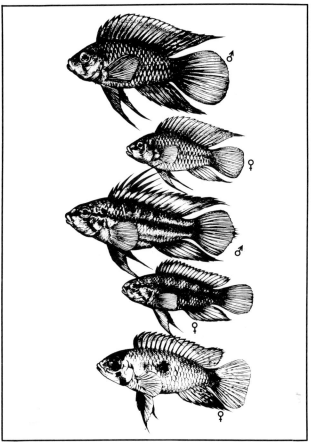

happens the first brood must be removed from the tank, otherwise the parents will regard them not only as competitors, but also as enemies and will attack them.

The dwarf cichlids of the genus *Apistogramma* reach a length of 6–8 cm (2¼–3 in). The best known are Ramirez's dwarf cichlid *(Apistogramma ramirezi)*, Agassiz's dwarf cichlid *(A. agassizi)*, the yellow dwarf cichlid *(A. reitzigi)* and also *A. cacatuoides* and *A. wickleri*. They come from the northern and central parts of South America and can be kept in water with a hardness not exceeding 10° DH, at a temperature of about 24°C (75°F), but a little higher if they are to be bred. It is important to have an acid pH, and this can be obtained by filtering the water through peat. It is also advisable to renew a proportion of the water at frequent intervals. In general, the dwarf cichlids are more delicate than their larger relatives and more demanding in their requirements; they are particularly sensitive to chemicals in the water. In the wild, the species of *Apistogramma* live a secluded life in waters that provide good shelter, so their aquarium tank should have roots and rocks arranged to provide sufficient hiding-places, and fairly dense marginal vegetation. There should be an open space for swimming in the centre of the tank. These fishes are more or less omnivorous.

For breeding it is naturally important to find a compatible pair. The sexes are easy to distinguish as the males are larger, more beautifully coloured and have more elongate fins. Generally the eggs are laid in a small cavity which has been carefully cleaned. In *A. ramirezi* both

from above:
Apistogramma reitzigi, male above, female below
Apistogramma cacatuoides, male above, female below
Apistogramma wickleri, female

Tank for dwarf cichlids, with flat and round rocks arranged to provide small caves. Shelter is also given by a large root and by the plants, mainly *Echinodorus* spp.

parents take part in looking after the brood, but in the other species this is done by the female. The eggs hatch after three to four days and the young can be fed on *Artemia* nauplii, finely chopped whiteworms, and *Tubifex*, as well as on fine powdered food.

In contrast to these dwarfs, the oscar or velvet cichlid *(Astronotus ocellatus)* is a true giant. Although offered on the market when about 2–4 cm ($\frac{3}{4}$–1$\frac{1}{2}$ in) long, this South American species can grow up to 35 cm (13$\frac{1}{2}$ in) in length, although it may be sexually mature at about 10 cm (3$\frac{3}{4}$ in). Adults or even half-grown specimens will begin to re-arrange the tank to their own liking. At this stage these cichlids are no longer suitable for a community tank and they must be given an aquarium on their own with plenty of shelter. Floating plants at the surface will help to diffuse the light and the bottom can be covered with a layer of medium-fine sand that is not too thick. Velvet cichlids are large, robust fishes that are rather difficult to breed. The sexes are not easy to distinguish with any degree of certainty. Courtship is extremely lively and the female sometimes suffers from the driving of the male. If the male chases the female too hard they

Apistogramma ramirezi

Apistogramma ramirezi

Astronotus ocellatus, normal form

should be separated, possibly by a pane of glass. The breeding tank should not be too small and its glass must be strong. When both sexes are seen to be cleaning a rock together this is a sign that they are likely to spawn successfully.

Velvet cichlids are usually kept in soft to medium-hard water at a temperature of 26°C (79°F), but this should be raised to 28°C (82°F) for breeding. When the eggs hatch both parents bring the young to a previously prepared pit, where they remain until they are free-swimming. A shoal of young from *A. ocellatus* may be very large, sometimes up to a thousand. However, the larger young eat the smaller, and eventually only 200–300 offspring may remain, but even this is too many for the average aquarist, for they are voracious feeders. It is only fairly recently that breeders have produced a coppery-red form of this cichlid, which is known as the red oscar. It can be kept in exactly the same way as the main species.

Another very interesting member of the cichlid family is the firemouth *(Cichlasoma meeki)*, which grows to 15 cm (6 in) in length and comes from Guatemala and Yucatan; it becomes sexually mature when 10 cm (3¾ in) long. These fishes live up to their popular name when displaying, with the gill-covers spread and the bottom of the mouth showing a brilliant red colour. They are not difficult to keep, in a tank with a minimum length of 80 cm (32 in). Like so many of its relatives the firemouth cichlid likes to dig up the bottom of the tank. Medium-fine sand mixed with fine gravel will therefore provide a suitable substrate. Any rocks and roots must be firmly fixed. Firemouths do not appear to have any requirements as regards the quality of the water, and the temperature can be in the region of 22–24°C (72–75°F). Any vegetation in the tank should be planted round the edges only as decoration, and the roots should be anchored down with rocks. Firemouth cichlids will eat any kind of live food, including earthworms, as well as dried, freeze-dried and deep-frozen food.

The male firemouth is normally somewhat larger than the female, and has brighter coloration. The species can be bred if a compatible pair can be found and placed in a separate breeding tank. Both sexes start by cleaning an area on the bottom. The female normally lays 300–400 eggs and these are protected and fanned by both parents. They hatch after about two days and the fry are taken to a pit. The young become free-swimming about eight days after hatching and they must then be given plenty of food, such as *Artemia* and *Cyclops* nauplii and finely divided powdered food. The parents continue to tend them for about four weeks.

Tank for large cichlids, with large, heavy rocks, a substrate of coarse gravel, a well-anchored root, firmly planted vegetation, and a few floating plants

left: *Astronotus ocellatus*, selected form known as the red oscar

Cichlasoma meeki

Cichlasoma octofasciatum

The Jack Dempsey *(Cichlasoma octofasciatum)* comes from the middle Amazon area and grows to a length of 20 cm (7¾ in). As the popular name suggests this is an aggressive species, best kept at a temperature of 20–22°C (68–72°F), which should be raised to 26°C (79°F) for breeding. The young fishes are grey with only a few small blue spots.

Cichlasoma cyanoguttatum

Cichlasoma nigrofasciatum

The Rio Grande perch *(Cichlasoma cyano-guttatum)* prefers slightly cooler water. It comes from Mexico and the southern parts of North America, growing to a length of 30 cm (12 in), but to only 10–20 cm (4–8 in) in the aquarium. These aggressive fishes require a tank with a minimum length of 120 cm (45 in), furnished with rocks, including some flat stones which should be placed in the centre. The quality of the water is not very important and it can be kept at room temperature, but not below 18°C (64°F); for breeding this should be raised to 24°C (75°F). These fishes consume a lot of food, and this of course tends to foul the water, so a proportion should be renewed at frequent intervals. The basic substrate can be a mixture of equal parts of medium-fine sand and fine gravel. The sexes can be distinguished only when the fishes are quite old, when the males start to develop a prominent bump on the forehead. Care must be taken when making up a pair. Spawning will normally take place on a large flat stone and several hundred young may be produced. In general, the habits of this species resemble those of the preceding species.

The zebra or convict cichlid *(Cichlasoma nigrofasciatum)* is another fairly small but aggressive species from Central America, where it lives in some of the lakes in Guatemala. It grows to 10 cm ($3\frac{3}{4}$ in) but can breed at 8 cm (3 in). Unlike most species of *Cichlasoma*, zebra cichlids can be kept in a group, provided the tank is at least 100 cm (40 in) long. They like to dig in the substrate, which should be soft sand, and they need some places to hide away in. Plants will almost certainly be uprooted, unless they are anchored down in suitable pots. Zebra cichlids are voracious, and they like to feed on snails. The sexes can be distinguished, for the male has elongated tips to the dorsal and anal fins. The water temperature should be 22–24°C (72–75°F), but a few degrees higher when breeding is attempted.

Salvin's cichlid *(Cichlasoma salvini)* grows to a length of 15 cm (6 in) and comes from southern Mexico, Guatemala and Honduras. It is a very beautiful species, particularly during courtship and when tending the young. Like most of the Central American cichlids, this species can tolerate lower temperatures for short periods, but not

Cichlasoma salvini, showing breeding coloration

below 20°C (68°F), and for breeding a few degrees higher. During courtship and the subsequent stages of breeding, Salvin's cichlid is extremely aggressive towards other fishes.

The banded cichlid *(Cichlasoma severum)* comes from Guyana and the Amazon basin. In its natural waters it reaches a length of 20 cm (7¾ in), but is usually rather less in the aquarium; it becomes sexually mature at about 10 cm (3¾ in). These are peaceful fishes which do, however, become aggressive during the breeding period. The tank should have a few firmly fixed rocks and a substrate consisting of a mixture of medium-fine sand and fine gravel. With most of these larger cichlids it is advisable to remove and wash the substrate at intervals and to renew the water. This is because the fishes consume

above: *Nannacara anomala*
below: *Herotilapia multispinosa*

such a large amount of food and produce so much faeces that the quality of the water is altered. A few tough plants, such as species of *Echinodorus* and *Vallisneria*, can be used, and they should grow.

These cichlids are relatively easy to feed when young, but as they grow older they will require much food, including such items as finely chopped meat or heart, the soft parts of bivalve molluscs, earthworms and so forth. The water temperature should be about 25°C (77°F).

Banded cichlids can be bred in the aquarium. The dorsal and anal fins have more elongated tips in the male than in the female. It is a good idea to rear a small shoal and wait until they start to form compatible pairs. Spawning takes place on the bottom and the young are tended by both parents. After they have consumed the contents of the yolk sac the fry can be given nauplii of *Artemia* and *Cyclops* for the first few days, and they will soon be able to take larger food.

The species of the genera *Crenicara* and *Nannacara* come from South America. The rare *Crenicara filamentosa* grows to about 10 cm (3¾ in) in length, and is not always easy to keep. The golden-eyed dwarf cichlid *(Nannacara anomala)* is smaller and not at all difficult. As in most of the small cichlids the females are a little smaller than the males. These cichlids require soft to medium-hard water (not exceeding 12° DH) kept at 24–26°C (75–79°F). They establish territories but are generally quite peaceful. The tank can be furnished with rocks, roots, a few plants and a substrate of fine gravel. One or two flat round stones should be half buried in the gravel, and these will provide a spawning site.

If the tank is large enough it can house one fully adult male and several females. In these small cichlids the male will often mate with more than one female. When the male has found a willing partner he starts scrupulously to clean the chosen area of substrate. In this species of *Nannacara* the female guards and tends the eggs and later also looks after the young. She keeps the male at a distance and will drive him off if he approaches too closely. At this point it is a good idea to remove the male from the tank. As in some of the other species the parent fish 'chews' the eggs to release the fry, which then gather in a pit on the bottom. They are free-swimming after a few days and are then led round by the female. They can now be fed on *Artemia* nauplii, on *Cyclops* (in moderation) and on powdered food. They develop a good appetite and grow rapidly.

A species only recently introduced into the aquarium is *Herotilapia multispinosa* in which the males grow to about 14 cm (5½ in) in length, the female remaining some 2 cm (¾ in) shorter. These fishes come from some of the lakes in Central America. They should be kept in a tank with a minimum length of 80 cm (32 in) holding about 200 litres (44 gallons). It can be furnished with rocks, large plants, and a flowerpot laid on its side to provide shelter. These fishes breed rapidly in the aquarium and are prolific, a brood of 1000 eggs being not uncommon.

Cichlids of the genus *Geophagus* differ in several respects from others living in South and Central America. They can be divided into two groups: substrate spawners and mouthbrooders. The latter have a highly specialized pattern of behaviour, of a type well known in some of the African cichlids. In *Geophagus*, the species *G. balzani*, *G. jurupari* and *G. surinamensis* are mouthbrooders, while the others are substrate spawners. The name *Geophagus* means 'earth-eaters', and refers to their habit of chewing, but not actually eating, the substrate. The best

Geophagus jurupari

known species is *Geophagus jurupari*, which comes from northern Brazil and grows to a length of 25 cm (9¾ in).

The tank can be furnished with darkish rocks and pieces of root and a few well-anchored plants. The water should be kept at about 26°C (79°F), and in any case the temperature should never be allowed to drop below 22°C (72°F). These fishes can be fed on small worms, including a few *Tubifex*, and on mosquito larvae and water-fleas.

The angelfishes, which also belong to the cichlid family, are certainly among the best-known and most popular aquarium fishes. There are three main species kept by aquarists, in addition to several selected, almost domesticated forms, including some with a marbled pattern on the flanks and others with elongated veil-like fins. For all these fishes the tank must be fairly large. The commonest species, *Pterophyllum scalare*, from the Amazon basin and Guyana, should be kept in a tall tank with some rockwork and a tangle of roots, and with plenty of vegetation. Although angelfishes can be kept in almost any kind of water, they will do best in soft water,

above: *Pterophyllum altum*

below: *Pterophyllum scalare*, normal form
below right: *Pterophyllum scalare*, a selected mottled form

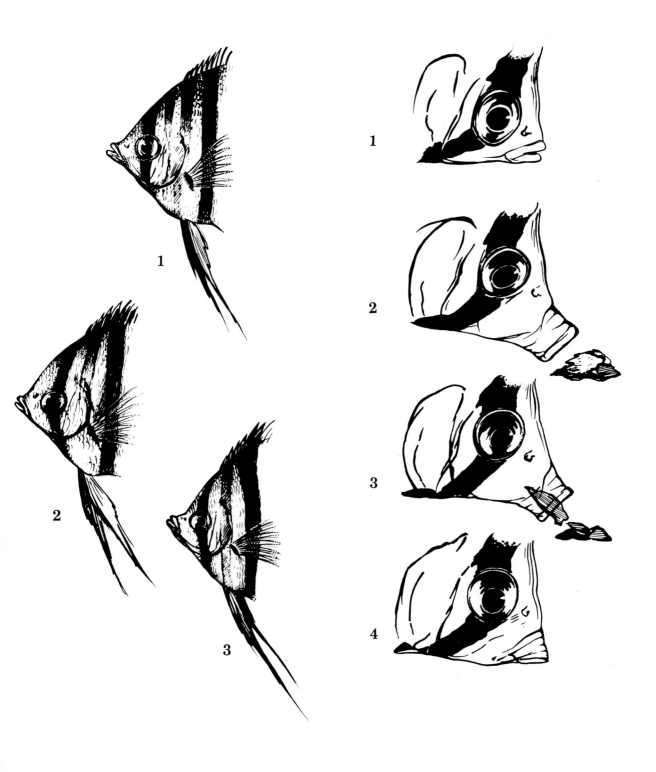

The three species of *Pterophyllum* can be distinguished by the shape of the head:
1 *P. dumerilii*
2 *P. scalare*
3 *P. altum*

Method of feeding in *Pterophyllum*:
1 the food is seen
2 the mouth is protruded
3 the food is sucked in
4 the mouth returns to its original position

A pair of discus fishes

Symphysodon aequifasciata aequifasciata

Sand banks in the Rio Negro

A fish-catching station on a sand bank

kept at a temperature of about 24°C (75°F). They have a good appetite and can be fed on *Tubifex*, whiteworms, mosquito larvae, *Cyclops* and water-fleas. They are also very fond of young fishes, especially newly born livebearers. Angel-fishes kept in a community tank often have their fins nibbled by other species, particularly by barbs, and they are perhaps better kept as a shoal in a separate species tank.

The other species kept in captivity are *P. altum*

and *P. dumerilii*, the former being imported more abundantly in recent years than the latter. *P. altum*, from the Orinoco and some of its tributaries, has an exceedingly tall body and a mouth which is turned upwards. If kept in a tank that is too small and with little shelter, these fishes become very nervous.

Angelfishes are not easy to sex, although their behaviour can give some clue. They breed fairly freely, sometimes even in a community tank, provided they are not disturbed. The parent fishes guard the eggs and later the young until they are free-swimming. They should then be separated from the other inmates of the tank.

The discus fishes form another small group of extremely attractive South American cichlids, but they are rather difficult to keep. They require very soft water (hardness 1–5° DH) with a pH of 6.2 to 6.6, or even less. Discus fishes are very susceptible to the attacks of various parasites, including the flagellate protozoan *Hexamita (= Octomitus)*. The microscopic organisms multiply in enormous numbers in the gut and then invade other organs. Gill flukes also attack discus fishes, and affect their respiration. They can be treated with Bayer's drug Masoten, using 0.5 mg per litre, and repeating this treatment eight days later. The water temperature should be kept at 28 C (82°F) during treatment.

Discus fishes come from the River Amazon and its tributaries. There are two species, namely *Symphysodon discus*, known as the discus, which comes mainly from the northern parts of the Rio Negro, and *S. aequifasciata*, with a distribution extending from the mouth of the Amazon upstream to the frontier with Colombia and Peru. Populations in the lower Amazon consist of fishes which are mainly brown, but from the middle Amazon upwards there are fishes with blue and green wavy lines on the flanks. The species *S. aequifasciata* has, in fact, been subdivided into three subspecies: the brown discus (*S. a. axelrodi*), lower Amazon from Belem to Manacapuru; the blue discus (*S. a. haraldi*), from the Amazon in the vicinity of Manacapuru; and the green discus (*S. a. aequifasciata*), upper Amazon from Tefé to the Colombian and Peruvian borders, and in the Rio Putumayo. There are also a few selected forms, including the turquoise discus which has been produced in Fort Lauderdale, Florida by Jack Wattley.

Typical habitat of the discus *(Symphysodon discus)* at Igarapé Curubau, near the entry of the Rio Branco into the Rio Negro

Another selected form of turquoise discus

The tank for discus fishes must be sufficiently large, with not less than 50–80 litres (10–18 gallons) of water per fish. Breeders keep a single pair in 300–400 litres (65–90 gallons). If the aquarist wants to have a substrate with plants it is advisable to make a shallow plastic tray to fit the bottom area of the tank. This can be made of PVC that will not release toxic materials into the water. The substrate and plants can be put into the tray, which can then be removed when cleaning the tank. Pieces of roots can be arranged in such a way that the fishes can shelter beneath them. Discus fishes can be fed on *Tubifex* and certain transparent mosquito larvae, but they apparently do not do so well on water-fleas, bloodworms or small *Cyclops*.

Provided the conditions are absolutely correct it should be possible to breed discus fishes,

The turquoise discus, a selected form

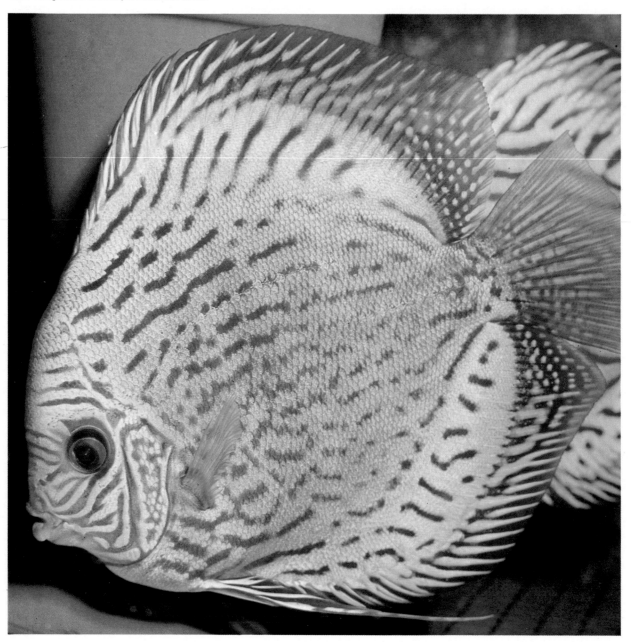

The turquoise discus
produced by Jack Wattley
of Florida

Symphysodon aequifasciata axelrodi

Symphysodon aequifasciata haraldi

Uaru amphiacanthoides

but this is a task to be attempted only by the advanced aquarist. The sexes are difficult to distinguish, and the fishes must be watched continuously, in order to pick up clues from their behaviour. They normally spawn on a hard substrate. After hatching, the young remain near the bottom until they have consumed the contents of their yolk sac and are free-swimming. They then move to the flanks of the parent fishes where they feed by 'grazing' a skin secretion. After a period they start to move away and to take small live food, such as *Artemia* nauplii. It may then be difficult to produce sufficient food of the correct type and size to keep the young fishes in good condition as they grow.

There is one other South American cichlid

An underwater scene in the rocky zone of Lake Malawi

The same locality seen at the surface

which, like the discus fishes, is much sought after and commands high prices. This is *Uaru amphiacanthoides*, which comes from the Amazon basin and Guyana. Adults can reach a length of 30 cm (11¾ in) but one never sees any of this size in the aquarium. These are peaceful fishes which require quiet company, so they could be kept with discus fishes. They also like the same type of soft, acid water, at the same temperature. *Uaru* can be bred, but the young are rather difficult to rear; they are very dark and only acquire the full coloration at sexual maturity.

We may now consider some of the African cichlids, and here we must distinguish between those that come from the central African lakes (mainly Lakes Malawi and Tanganyika), and those from the rivers of eastern, western and central Africa. In contrast to the river species, the lake cichlids cannot extend their natural distribution range, and this has led to the development of all kinds of ecological niches and unusual forms of specialization. Some have evolved mouths adapted for rasping algae off steep underwater cliffs, at the same time taking the small invertebrates living there, others feed on the scales of other fishes and even on the eyes of other fishes *(Haplochromis compressiceps)*. One of these specialists is *Hemitilapia oxyrhynchus*, which feeds on algae, which it grazes from leaves and elsewhere. In the aquarium, however, where there is no shortage of food, this natural behaviour is not observed.

Very clear water in Lake Tanganyika

Haplochromis sp., possibly *H. ahli*

Among the substrate spawners both parents share the work more or less equally, but in the mouthbrooders there is a division of labour, for the male does the preliminary work, digging out the spawning pit and starting the courtship, whereas the female takes over brood protection after the eggs have been laid. The mouthbrooder *Haplochromis burtoni* is a striking representative of these African cichlids. It requires a tank

Haplochromis burtoni

with dense marginal vegetation, and rocks and roots arranged to provide hiding-places. These fishes should be kept in a separate species tank with a substrate of fine sand. The water should be at a temperature of 23–25°C (73–77°F) but the composition is not of great importance. The fishes will take all kinds of live food, including small earthworms, and also chopped mussel flesh.

The anal fin of the male is marked with what are known as egg dummies. After spawning the female quickly takes the eggs into her mouth, before they have been fertilized. The male now swims back and forth in front of her mouth, waiting for an opportunity to shed his sperm over the eggs. The female snaps at the egg dummies on his anal fin, and in so doing she naturally opens her mouth. At this moment the male sheds sperm which are drawn into her mouth, where they fertilize the eggs. After hatching, the young spend a short period using up the contents of their yolk sac, and then become free-swimming, but they still remain under the protection of the female. At this stage they can be fed on *Artemia* nauplii.

Haplochromis moorii

Haplochromis euchilus

Another mouthbrooding species, *Haplochromis polystigma*, comes from Lake Malawi, and even in an aquarium it may reach a length of 20 cm ($7\frac{3}{4}$ in). These fishes should be kept in water with a hardness of 12–16° DH, and at a temperature of about 24°C (75°F). The young, which are a marbled grey, have a good appetite and soon grow into large, iridescent-blue predators. They should not, therefore, be kept in a community tank. They will even eat fishes of their own species, so it is advisable to furnish the tank with plenty of rocks and roots to provide hiding-places. They can be fed on a diet of chopped heart, earthworms and young fishes. Breeding takes place as in *H. burtoni* and the anal fin of the male also has egg dummies. The young are not difficult to rear. By the time they have left the mouth of the mother they have already reached a length of 1 cm ($\frac{1}{3}$ in) and have a relatively large mouth. They can take small pieces of *Tubifex* and young water-fleas.

One of the most attractive of the Lake Malawi mouthbrooding cichlids is *Haplochromis moorii*, which is a brilliant blue, a colour not found in such intensity in river cichlids. This species grows to a length of 20 cm ($7\frac{3}{4}$ in), and unlike others in which only the male develops a protruding forehead, here the female also does so. This fish is found only in Lake Malawi where it lives not in rocky areas, but on sandy bottoms. It is a good idea to keep this species with other fishes that burrow in the bottom, for in so doing they release small particles of food of which *H. moorii* is very fond.

Aulonocara nyassae

Haplochromis polystigma

Another cichlid from Lake Malawi, *Aulonocara nyassae*, lives in the transitional zone between rocks and sand. It reaches a length of about 18 cm (7 in), but less in the aquarium, and is capable of breeding at a length of 8 cm (3 in). The males show brilliant blue and red colours but the females remain grey-brown. These fishes are also mouthbrooders, the eggs being laid usually in small caves. Like most of the African lake cichlids this species requires water that is more or less the opposite of what the South American cichlids need, namely medium-hard to hard with a pH around 8. The tank should have rockwork that provides a few caves.

Finally, there is the largish mouthbrooder *Haplochromis euchilus*, up to about 20 cm ($7\frac{3}{4}$ in) in length, which also comes from Lake Malawi. In the wild these fishes feed by rasping algal growths with their large fleshy lips. These are relatively peaceful fishes which breed in the same way as the other Malawi species mentioned. The sexes are easily distinguished, as there are egg dummies on the anal fin of the male.

The red cichlid or jewel fish (*Hemichromis bimaculatus*) is an attractive but aggressive species that is well worth keeping in a tank on its own, where it is not difficult to breed. Red cichlids come from northern tropical Africa where they reach a length of about 18 cm (7 in), but only about 12 cm ($4\frac{3}{4}$ in) in the aquarium. Several individuals should be kept in a sufficiently large tank. They will soon establish territories, and

Hemichromis bimaculatus

Hemichromis bimaculatus, in breeding coloration, with young

it should then be possible to distinguish the pairs. The tank can be furnished with rocks and roots to divide up the area, and with small caves built into the rear wall. It is best not to have any plants, but if there are any they must be very robust forms, such as *Vallisneria* and *Echinodorus*. The substrate can be a mixture of medium-fine sand and medium gravel, with a flat round stone to serve as a spawning site. The water composition is not very critical, but the temperature should be kept at 22–24°C (72–75°F). These fishes develop a good appetite, and in addition to various live foods they can be offered scraped heart, earthworms and occasionally fish flesh.

During the breeding season red cichlids develop characteristic brilliant red coloration, particularly on the belly. At other times the back is olive to grey-brown and the belly yellowish, and there are dark blotches on the gill covers. The sexes are difficult to distinguish, but the female is usually stouter, with more brilliant red coloration during the breeding season. The almost continuous territorial fighting should be carefully watched by the aquarist and the tank population gradually reduced by removing all except the most active pair, which give the appearance of being compatible. These two fishes will now start to look for a suitable substrate for spawning, and they will probably choose the flat stone already positioned in the foreground of the tank. They then clean the upper surface of the stone, and during this operation they repeatedly rub their bellies against it, possibly to loosen any algae. It may be several hours or even days before the female finally spawns. The male immediately fertilizes the eggs, which may number about four hundred. The fry hatch after forty-eight hours and are taken by both parents to a previously prepared and well-sheltered pit. Both parents swim around the brood, protecting them most assiduously. The young will have consumed their yolk sac in about two days and they can then be fed on very fine live food, offered in large quantities. Feeding with *Artemia* nauplii will only suffice for a transitional period, and the young will soon require the next size of live food, e.g. *Cyclops*.

A second member of this genus, the five-spot cichlid or banded jewelfish *(Hemichromis fasciatus)*, is perhaps the most aggressive of all the

Hemichromis fasciatus

cichlids. It comes from West Africa and grows to a length of 25–28 cm (9¾–11 in). Five-spot cichlids establish territories in the lower water layers of the tank. Although extremely aggressive towards one another when adult or even half-grown, they are most tender in the care of the young. They are, of course, quite unsuitable for a community tank, but should be kept in a separate species tank furnished with rocks, roots and very tough, robust plants.

Lake Tanganyika, with a depth of over 1400 metres (c. 4590 feet), is one of the deepest lakes in the world. A great many of the fish species living there are endemic, that is, they are found nowhere else. *Lamprologus* is one of the cichlid genera represented in this lake. Most of its species have a very large mouth and are predatory. Two species worth mentioning are *L. brichardi* (formerly *L. savoryi elongatus*) and the larger *L. compressiceps*.

Lamprologus brichardi, which grows to a length of 10 cm (3¾ in), spawns in caves, almost always attaching its eggs to the roof. After hatching, the young remain in a little shoal in front of the cave and are protected by both parents, but particularly by the male. He positions himself at the boundary of his territory and chases off any fish which tries to cross this boundary, ramming most aggressively and even biting. The water should have a hardness of 10–15° DH and a pH of about 8. At Burundi, on the shores of Lake Tanganyika, the water was found to have a hardness of 11° DH and a pH of 9. So in the aquarium, water with a pH of 8 will do no harm to the fishes. It was on this occasion that the photograph below of a freshly caught

L. compressiceps with the dorsal fin fully erected, was taken. This species, usually photographed with the dorsal fin folded, lives hidden among dense vegetation, ready to rush out and catch prey in the deeply cleft mouth.

During recent years the cichlids of the African lakes have become very popular. This is not surprising, for not only do they show very interesting behaviour patterns, but many are also extremely colourful. Indeed they are sometimes known as 'freshwater coralfishes'. At the present time the best known genera appear to be *Labeotropheus, Pseudotropheus, Melanochromis* and *Tropheus*. The species kept in the aquarium include *Pseudotropheus zebra*, which occurs in more than one colour form, *P. microstoma, M. auratus*, as well as *Labeotropheus trewavasae* and *L. fuelleborni*. These species all come from Lake Malawi. From Lake Tanganyika come the mouthbrooding species *Tropheus moorii* and *T. duboisi*.

These fishes, as well as others not mentioned here, are extremely territorial, and can therefore only be kept in a tank with a minimum length of 100 cm (40 in). The water should on no account be too soft and must have a hardness of

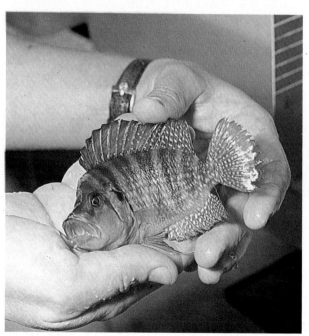

Lamprologus compressiceps, with dorsal fin erected

Lamprologus brichardi

Tropheus moorii

at least 10° DH. The pH is also important, and it should always be alkaline (above pH 7). In both lakes the temperature fluctuates seasonally within the range 24–30°C (75–86°F). Observations in Lake Tanganyika have shown that these fishes never live more than a short distance from the steep, underwater cliffs. In the aquarium, therefore, the rear wall can be covered with rockwork that extends right to the water surface. Although plants might add to the aesthetic appeal of such a tank, it is not really advisable to have them. In the wild many of these lake cichlids have very specialized food habits, but in the aquarium they will eat almost anything, including the usual live foods, trout pellets, chopped liver or heart, with a regular supplement of greenstuff.

The lake cichlids show some variation in their breeding habits, but here we will deal only with *Pseudotropheus zebra* from Lake Malawi, a species which has several colour variants. These include blue-black banded males, various spotted forms, which are usually females, and some individuals that are pale blue or almost bluish-white. It is possible that more than one species is represented in this assemblage. This

Melanochromis auratus, male above, female below

Labeotropheus trewavasae, yellow female

Labeotropheus trewavasae, blue male

view is supported by the fact that males belonging to different colour variants, e.g. blue-blacks and pure blues, do not fight one another.

Courtship is often quite strenuous. After a few sham matings the female lays her eggs on the substrate, sometimes in a small pit, and immediately takes them into her mouth. There they are fertilized by the male, who exhibits the egg dummies on his anal fin to make the female open her mouth and receive the sperm, a technique already described above for *Haplochromis burtoni*. The female retains the brood within her mouth for about four weeks, before allowing the young fishes to leave. During this period she takes little or no food. After the young have become independent of the female, they start to show a certain amount of inborn aggression, for each one establishes a small territory which it defends most vigorously. At this stage they can be given finely divided food, which they will consume in large quantities, and grow rapidly.

Some of the beautiful *Julidochromis* species are imported from Lake Tanganyika. The basic ground coloration is mostly yellowish, marked with various patterns of black stripes, spots and blotches. The fin edges are often a bright blue. These fishes all have an elongated body and an oval cross section. They live in areas with rocks and a sandy bottom, and the females spawn in caves. The imported species include *Julidochromis marlieri*, *J. ornatus*, *J. regani* and *J. transcriptus*. These fishes grow to a length of 12–15 cm (4¾–6 in). In 1975 a further species was found at the southern end of Lake Tanganyika. This is *J.*

dickfeldi, which has rather different coloration from the other species; it has already been bred.

Like the other lake cichlids, those from Lake Tanganyika must not be given soft water. Fin twitching and abnormal swimming are signs that the water is too soft, and in this respect the young fishes are particularly sensitive. The adults do not usually grow to their full size in the aquarium. The water should have a hardness of 12–18° DH, a pH of 7.5–8.5, and a temperature of about 24°C (75°F). Lake Tanganyika cichlids also require a tank with plenty of shelter, as each individual and each pair defends a territory. A few isolated plants can be used, with plenty of space in between them so that the interesting behaviour of the fishes can be properly observed. These fishes must be given a high proportion of live food, as they will not thrive on dried food alone. They appear to be stimulated by the movements of the food animals. They have a relatively small mouth and cannot therefore eat large pieces of food.

The female lays her eggs on the roof of a cave and both parents guard the brood. The eggs hatch after about three days and the young fishes will be completely free-swimming after a further six days. They remain for another week in the little cave and then gradually start to leave it. The individual broods consist of only twenty to thirty eggs, often fewer. The parent fishes may spawn again a few weeks later, so it is not abnormal to see broods of different ages swimming in the vicinity of the spawning site. Young fishes that are half-grown but in full

Julidochromis ornatus

Julidochromis marlieri

coloration will be chased from the territory by the parents, and should therefore be removed from the tank, unless it is a very large one.

The genus *Pelmatochromis* comprises a group of small cichlids from West Africa. They are very difficult to identify. In 1968 one expert in the field thought that there were no fewer than twenty-five species in the genus and he suggested a new genus, *Pelvicachromis*, for some of them. In 1973, Dr Ethelwynn Trewavas retained only three species in the genus *Pelmatochromis*.

In their home area these cichlids live in fresh waters close to the coasts of West Africa. *Pelmatochromis thomasi*, a lively, territorial but peaceful small cichlid grows to a length of 10 cm

Julidochromis dickfeldi

Julidochromis regani

(2¾ in); the female sometimes a little more. Like so many others, this species requires plenty of hiding-places constructed out of rocks and stones, but it is not demanding as regards the composition of the water. In its home range, acid river waters mix with harder coastal waters to give medium hardness. It is therefore appropriate to add a little sea salt, about 2 table-spoonfuls to 10 litres (2.2 gallons) of tank water. The colours become more beautiful when the

Pelvicachromis pulcher, formerly known as *Pelmatochromis kribensis*

fishes are kept in such slightly brackish water. The temperature should be about 25°C (77°F). These fishes need a diet consisting mainly of live food, with some dried food.

The different *Pelmatochromis* species vary considerably in the form of the body and fins. With the exception of *P. thomasi*, all the males have the dorsal fin prolonged to end in a point. The species are not too difficult to breed, and indeed they will often do so in a community tank. However, when this happens the parents will have a difficult task guarding the young from so many potential enemies. Spawning is not the same in all the species. Some lay their eggs on the roof of small caves, but others such as *P. thomasi* prefer to use a flat stone as a spawning substrate. In some instances the fishes will spawn on leaves, or on flowerpots and pieces of coconut shell. The eggs hatch in about three days and the young become free-swimming soon afterwards. In all species they are guarded by both parents. The young can be fed on live food, starting with the nauplii of *Artemia* and *Cyclops*.

Most of the species known to aquarists as belonging to the genus *Pelmatochromis* have now been transferred to *Pelvicachromis*. The best known is *Pelvicachromis pulcher*, from southern

A tributary of the River Zaïre (formerly Congo) with fast-flowing water

Steatocranus casuarius

Nigeria, which was formerly known as *Pelmatochromis kribensis*. These fishes can be kept in the same way as *P. thomasi*.

Fishes that live in running water mostly have a torpedo-like body form adapted for this way of life. Among those that live in this type of habitat is the blockhead cichlid *(Steatocranus casuarius)* a fairly well known aquarium fish with a characteristic dome-shaped outgrowth on the head of the male. Others include *Nanochromis nudiceps*, *Steatocranus tinanti* and *Teleogramma brichardi*. These species reach a length of about 10 cm ($3\frac{3}{4}$ in) and come from the fast-flowing parts of the upper, middle and lower Congo (now River Zaire). They live in among rocks, roots and submerged branches, and their body form and behaviour patterns are ideally adapted for very unfavourable living conditions in waters which sometimes flow extremely rapidly. These fishes can be kept in water with a hardness of 10–15° DH, at a temperature of 24–26°C (75–79°F). Being river fishes, their tank water should be changed fairly frequently. They are peaceful and will not even destroy the plants, but will eat live and dried food.

Blockhead cichlids can be kept in a community tank, but it is better to keep them on their own. The tank should be at least 60 cm (24 in) long, and furnished with numerous holes and other places of shelter constructed from roots, bamboo canes or flowerpots. During courtship and spawning these cichlids become quite aggressive, and require a territory of about 0.25

sq m (c. ¼ sq. yd) around their retreat. Intruding fishes are usually pushed away and bitten. Young blockheads which have just become sexually mature may still be difficult to sex, although with increasing age the outgrowth on the head of the male becomes increasingly prominent. It is best to put about six young adults in a tank and allow them to sort themselves into one or more compatible pairs. The eggs, which are oval, greyish-white and about 3 mm (⅛ in) long, are laid and fertilized in the pair's retreat. The parent fishes share the task of brood protection. The male keeps the territory free of intruders, while the female tends the eggs and young. Both parents can be seen leading the young fishes around the tank as soon as they have become free-swimming. At this stage they can be fed on very fine live food.

The African cichlid genus *Tilapia* has a large number of fishes which present numerous problems to the ichthyologists who try to name and classify them. They are distributed throughout Africa, with a few species extending into the Near East, and many species provide food for Africans living on lakes and rivers. Some species have even been introduced into other continents

Tilapia mossambica

as a source of food. The best known of these is the Mozambique mouthbrooder *(Tilapia mossambica)* which has been taken to many parts of south-eastern Asia, and has even been introduced into brackish-water ponds in the Hawaiian Islands. Perhaps the most highly specialized member of the genus is *T. grahami* which lives in Lake Magadi, a soda lake in Kenya, where the water has a pH of 10.5 and a temperature fluctuating between 32° and 42°C (88–107°F).

Tilapia mossambica occurs naturally in East Africa, with a range extending from the Nile in the north to Natal in the south. It reaches a length of 30–40 cm (11¾–15¾ in), and is a mouthbrooder. These fishes can be kept only in a large tank, furnished with robust and heavy objects. The substrate can be coarse gravel, but there should be no plants, as the males dig deep pits at spawning time. The water should be medium-hard with a temperature of 22–24°C (72–75°F). The diet consists of all types of live and dead food. The males have a red border to the dorsal and caudal fins.

Tilapia mariae from West Africa, particularly the lower Niger, spawns on the bottom. These are fast-growing fishes which reach a length of up to 20 cm (7¾ in). The tank should be furnished in the same way as for *T. mossambica*. The sexes are easily distinguishable in the adults, for the males are larger, with more elongated, pointed dorsal and anal fins, and with a slight dome-shaped outgrowth on the forehead. They feed mainly on vegetation, but will take other foods.

Landing *Tilapia* for the market at the village of Vitshumbi (Zaïre), on Lake Idi Amin Dada

Mating of *Betta splendens*, seen through the glass bottom of an aquarium tank

Breeders have produced numerous colour variants of the fighting fish *(Betta)*

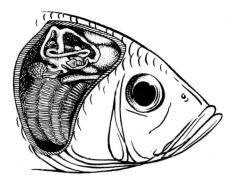

Head of an anabantid with part of the side cut away to show the labyrinth organ above the gills

Macropodus opercularis

Distribution of anabantids

Labyrinth fishes

The labyrinth fishes of the family Anabantidae occur in south-east Asia and in parts of Africa. They possess an accessory respiratory apparatus, known as the labyrinth organ, lying in the upper part of each gill chamber, behind the eyes. The organ consists of numerous, much-folded lamellae and it enables the fishes to breathe atmospheric air, in much the same way as lungs do in other vertebrates. The fishes can be seen coming to the surface to take in bubbles of air. This is an adaptation to life in muddy waters deficient in dissolved oxygen, and the fishes have become so highly adapted to this method of respiration that they cannot survive by gill respiration alone. In fact if they are denied access to the air above the water surface they will soon die.

At spawning time many species of Anabantidae build a bubble nest. In an area with little current the male comes to the surface and spits out bubbles of air coated with a mucus-like secretion. These bubbles remain at the surface forming the nest. During the subsequent spawning the male encircles the female's body and she lays the eggs. In some species the eggs float up to the nest owing to their content of oil, in others the male catches the eggs in his mouth and spits them into the nest. The male then guards the nest, from time to time adding new air bubbles. This keeps the eggs and their supporting air bubbles at, or even slightly above, the water surface. The eggs hatch in about two days and the young then live for a short period on the contents of their yolk sac. After this they start to take very fine live food, and the male begins to lose interest in them. At this stage a watch should be kept to ensure that the faster-growing young do not attack their siblings.

The paradisefish *(Macropodus opercularis)* is believed to have been the first tropical fish introduced into Europe for aquarium purposes; this was about the year 1876. It has a wide distribution, extending from China and Korea to Vietnam, and it grows to a length of 7–8 cm ($2\frac{3}{4}$–3 in) in the aquarium. Paradisefishes can be kept in a community tank, but they tend to become aggressive towards the other inmates, and are really more suitable for a separate species tank. The water should be medium-hard, at a temperature of about 24°C (75°F), and the tank

Betta splendens, a pair beneath their bubble nest

Betta splendens, two males fighting

should have dense vegetation, including some floating plants. The coloration of the fishes is usually brilliant red with numerous blackish transverse bars showing blue iridescence. The back is somewhat darker, the throat pale. The fins are much elongated and marked with a pattern of red, black and blue streaks and dots.

One of the best known members of this family is the fighting fish *(Betta splendens)*. The popular name refers to the exceedingly aggressive fighting of the males. When two of these are put together each will usually regard the whole tank as its own territory, and the ensuing fight may prove fatal. Fighting fishes are quite small, up to 6 cm (2¼ in) long, and although they can be kept in a community tank they are much better on their own. The tank need not be longer than 60 cm (24 in) and should be relatively shallow, with dense vegetation, including a few floating plants. The water can be soft to medium-hard at a temperature of about 26°C (79°F). The fishes will feed on all types of food. The sexes are easy to distinguish, as the females are smaller and without the much-developed fins that are characteristic of the males. Breeders have produced a number of different colour variants.

Other popular aquarium anabantids come from the genera *Colisa*, *Trichogaster* and *Trichopsis*. These include *Colisa chuna*, up to 4.5 cm (1¾ in) long, from Assam and Bangladesh, the dwarf gourami *(Colisa lalia)*, up to 5 cm (2 in) long, from the same area, the pearl gourami *(Trichogaster leeri)*, up to 14 cm (5½ in) long, from

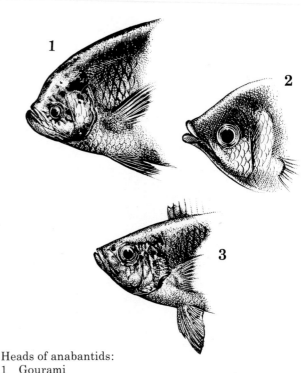

Heads of anabantids:
1 Gourami
2 Kissing gourami
3 Climbing perch

154

Betta splendens, three colour variants, all males

Colisa chuna

Colisa lalia

south-east Asia, and the croaking gourami *(Trichopsis vittatus)*, up to 6 cm (2¼ in) long, from the same region. These gouramis do well in a community tank, with medium-hard water, at a temperature not below 26°C (79°F), and they require a varied diet.

The kissing gourami *(Helostoma temmincki)* is another species from south-east Asia, growing to a length of up to 30 cm (11¾ in) in the aquarium, but it is really attractive only when much smaller. Most of them are whitish with a pink sheen, but there are reddish and greenish colour variants. The popular name of these fishes refers to the fleshy lips used for grazing algae, but also seen apparently to kiss when the fishes are indulging in sham fighting. They can be kept in almost any kind of water, at a temperature around 24°C (75°F), and the tank should have some dense vegetation and its area divided up by pieces of root.

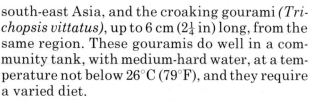

Helostoma temmincki, green and pink forms

Trichogaster leeri

top: *Trichogaster trichopterus*, selected form known as the
Cosby gourami
above: *Trichogaster trichopterus*, original form

Sphaerichthys osphromenoides

Ctenopoma acutirostre

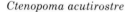

The chocolate gourami *(Sphaerichthys osphromenoides)*, from south-east Asia, grows only to a length of 5 cm (2 in). It was for a long time somewhat of a mystery in the aquarium world as regards its breeding habits, some saying it was a mouthbrooder, others a livebearer. This was largely because the species is not nearly so easy to keep or breed as the other aquarium anabantids. The natural habitat of the chocolate gourami is very different from that of the other species, for it requires very soft and acid water (hardness 0–3° DH and pH below 6). According to recent information these fishes do not build a bubble nest, but the female takes the eggs into her mouth after they have been fertilized. The species requires a high temperature (about 28°C or 82°F) and a varied diet which should include some insects, as this appears to stimulate breeding.

The African anabantids of the genus *Ctenopoma* are not so commonly kept in the home aquarium. Unlike most of their Asiatic relatives they are mostly aggressive predators which in the wild feed on small fishes and large insects. The spotted climbing perch *(Ctenopoma acutirostre)* from Zaire is an attractive fish, but it grows up to 15 cm (6 in) long, and so is rather large for the majority of home aquarium tanks. It must on no account be kept with smaller fishes, which it will chase and attack relentlessly. The tank should have dense vegetation and other opportunities for shelter, and the water should be medium-hard at a temperature of about 25°C (77°F). Besides taking small fishes, *Ctenopoma acutirostre* will also eat earthworms and mealworms, as well as other foods.

Sand smelts

The sand smelts (family Atherinidae) are mainly marine fishes, some of which have penetrated into estuaries, and there are some in fresh waters. A few of the latter have become good aquarium fishes, and these include the dwarf rainbowfish *(Melanotaenia maccullochi)* from northern Australia, which grows up to 8 cm (3 in) in length. These are peaceful fishes, which should be kept as a shoal in a well-lit tank with marginal vegetation and plenty of open water for swimming. The plants should be those with feathery leaves. The water can be medium-hard, at a temperature of about 24°C (75°F). Rainbow-fishes will eat all types of food.

Sticklebacks

The sticklebacks (family Gasterosteidae) provide one or two fishes suitable for the aquarium, which are particularly attractive during the breeding period. These are cold-water fishes. There are three main species in Europe, one of which is marine, and several in North America. Many of the sticklebacks that are found in fresh waters can also live in the sea. They have a varying number of sharp spines on the dorsal line, hence the popular name. These spines represent the front spiny-rayed dorsal fin of certain other fishes.

Gasterosteus aculeatus

Melanotaenia maccullochi

The three-spined stickleback *(Gasterosteus aculeatus)* is a common freshwater fish of Europe, and is also found in northern Asia, Japan and North America. It can be kept in a well-planted and well-lit tank with a water temperature of 16–20°C (61–68°F). If the temperature does tend to rise in summer, it should never be allowed to exceed 22°C (72°F). In winter the tank should be moved to an unheated room so that the temperature can sink to 5–10°C (41–50°F). This cool period in winter acts as a stimulus to the breeding drive in spring. The male builds a nest of plant fragments and entices a female to lay eggs in it. This process is repeated with other females, until the nest may contain hundreds of eggs. The male then chases away the last female and guards the nest until the eggs hatch. He continues to tend the young fishes for a further period, actively driving away any intruders from the nest area.

Tetraodon fluviatilis

Pufferfishes

The pufferfishes (family Tetraodontidae) are mainly marine, but a few live in brackish and fresh waters. The popular name refers to their ability to inflate themselves, so that they appear much larger than they really are, thus lessening their chance of being eaten. The green pufferfish *(Tetraodon fluviatilis)*, which occurs from India to the Philippines, is often available in aquarist shops, where it is seldom longer than 5 cm (2 in), although the species can grow up to 20 cm (7¾ in). The other species commonly available is *Tetraodon palembangensis* from southeast Asia.

Freshwater pufferfishes can be kept in a relatively large tank with a moderate amount of marginal vegetation, and rockwork built to provide small caves for shelter. The water must on

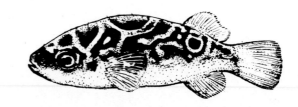

Tetraodon palembangensis

no account be soft, but should contain some sea salt, e.g. 3–4 teaspoonfuls to 10 litres (2.2 gallons) of water. The temperature should be 22–26°C (72–79°F). It is usually an advantage to keep pufferfishes in a separate tank without other species, but there must be numerous hiding-places, as these fishes are rather quarrelsome. They will eat grated heart and chopped liver as well as the usual live foods, and they are particularly fond of snails.

PART TWO
The Marine Aquarium

Introduction

This section of the book is primarily concerned with the maintenance of aquarium tanks for tropical marine fishes and invertebrates. Most of these animals are imported from the areas of coral reef which occur in the Indo-Pacific and in the Caribbean Sea, and many of them are highly specialized for life in this particular natural habitat.

Coral reefs occur on or near the coast. Those that run parallel to the coast are known as barrier reefs, the best known being the Great Barrier Reef off the east coast of Queensland, Australia. Like all coral formations these are the work of uncountable millions of tiny coral polyps, which belong to the phylum Coelenterata (corals, sea-anemones, jellyfishes). These small animals secrete calcium to form their skeletons. In addition most coral polyps contain microscopic algae, which help to colour the corals. Other algae live in between the coral stocks, and their calcareous secretions help to cement the reef. Both corals and algae require light, as well as warm, clear water rich in oxygen, hence they are found in a relatively narrow zone of tropical coastal surface waters.

Apart from the fishes themselves which are being imported in increasing numbers into Europe and North America, some living corals, or pieces of them, also appear on the market. These are extremely difficult to keep for any length of time and they cannot be recommended for any except the highly skilled specialist. The average aquarist must be content to decorate his tropical marine tank with the calcareous or horny skeletons of coral, after these have been thoroughly cleaned. In addition, some use what have been called 'living rocks', a term that will be explained below.

The complex structure of a coral reef provides excellent shelter not only for fishes, but also for a great variety of invertebrates, or animals without backbones. Like corals and algae, coral-reef fishes and the associated invertebrates have become highly adapted to living in bright light with fast-moving water rich in oxygen. These factors obviously present some problems to anyone who is trying to establish some semblance of the natural habitat in an aquarium tank. In addition there is the problem of supplying an adequate and varied diet to many different kinds of fishes and invertebrates.

The basic food supply in the sea is the plankton, a collective term for all the free-floating, mostly very small animals and plants. Some of these organisms remain afloat by reducing their specific gravity by storing fat or secreting gas. Others increase their surface area by the development of long thin processes, which slow down their rate of sinking. Planktonic plants include the diatoms, tiny green cells which float near the surface and provide food for a vast assortment of planktonic animals. Some of these animals are the larvae of animals living on the sea floor, whereas others are adults, albeit tiny ones, in their own right.

As an example of extreme specialization there is the cleaner wrasse, a small fish that removes parasites from the fishes. For, unlike many invertebrates such as shrimps, fishes cannot scratch themselves, although some can be seen

far left: *Zebrasoma xanthurum*
left: *Acanthurus olivaceus*

far left: *Amphiprion frenatus*
in a sea-anemone
left: *Amphiprion ephippium*
in a sea-anemone
(*Radianthus* sp.)

rubbing their body against rocks to get rid of unwanted parasites. This is where the cleaner wrasse comes in. Other fishes have been seen to open their mouths and spread their gill covers to allow the little wrasse access to places where parasites lodge, or to areas of loose skin. These the wrasse quickly cleans up, and in doing so it also acquires food. There is also a cleaner prawn which gives a similar service.

Another specialization involves symbiosis, a phenomenon in which two quite different animals live together. In the marine aquarium the best known case is the relationship between the clownfishes or anemone-fishes of the genus *Amphiprion* and certain large tropical sea-anemones, each deriving some benefit from the association.

Nowadays tropical marine fishes and invertebrates are caught in their native waters by professional collectors, who use highly sophisticated methods of packing and transport so that the animals normally arrive at their destination in excellent condition. Nevertheless, any aquarist buying marine tropicals should examine them very carefully with a lens. They should show no sign of injury or disease. In particular, the body and fins must be free of white spots or films, or of inflamed areas; the eyes should not be protruding, and the swimming movements should be normal. Many newly imported fishes will not have fed for some time, and this lowers their resistance to disease. A concave belly often denotes hunger, and anal inflammation suggests a digestive disorder.

Tanks and equipment

Sea water has a highly corrosive action on all metals; far more so than fresh water. At one time this was a serious problem for anyone attempting to keep marine organisms, for rust not only destroys metal tanks but it also has a damaging effect on fish life.

Nowadays, however, the tank presents few problems. Most marine aquarists would now buy an all-glass tank, in which the glass panes are cemented together with silicone rubber, which gives a practically indestructible joint. Those aquarists who want to construct their own tank could use asbestos-cement sheets as this is a reliable, easily worked material. In such a tank only the front is glass, and the other walls and the bottom should be carefully coated, when absolutely dry, with a good-quality epoxy resin. This not only reduces porosity, but it also prevents any possible toxins from leaching out of the cement.

Heaters for a marine tank should be made of glass, with a plastic cap that is resistant to sea water. Lighting should present no special difficulties, as there are several types on the market. The only trouble is that any fine bubbles from the aerator tend to accumulate on the lamp system, producing a crust of salt which soon causes trouble. There are, fortunately, other more appropriate ways of bringing air to the tank water.

All marine aquarium tanks will require some form of filtration, circulation and aeration. Filtration keeps the water clear and optically clean, while movement of the water by circulation, and its aeration, are quite essential for the well-being of the fishes and invertebrates, and also of any algae in the tank. Fortunately these requirements are met by a submerged centrifugal pump, which removes particles of detritus from the water, draws in fresh air, and continually circulates the water, thus imitating on

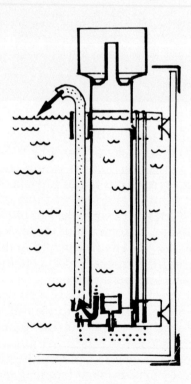

A protein skimmer helps to remove organic waste from the aquarium water

a small scale much of what happens on the open reef.

A foam filter or protein skimmer does a job which most pumps cannot really perform. This is the removal of some of the organic waste, mostly of an albuminous nature. It works on a very simple principle, using the ability of the polluted water to form a foam. The water is taken into a container where it is mixed with air. The resulting foam rises up into a detachable receiver at the top, which is outside the tank circulation. The foam accumulated in this receiver is discarded at intervals. In this way much of the organic waste matter is removed from the tank. Ozone (a form of oxygen with three linked oxygen atoms) can also be used in conjunction with a protein skimmer. The ozone, produced by an ozonizer, is mixed with the air entering the protein skimmer, and this is said to increase the latter's efficiency.

Some aquarists use ultra-violet radiation to kill bacteria, but this requires some thought and care. Certain bacteria perform an important service in the aquarium. In a properly maintained tank the aerobic bacteria, requiring oxygen, break down organic waste substances into water, carbon dioxide and mineral salts, so it would be a mistake to kill them. On the other hand anaerobic bacteria (which work without oxygen) produce undesirable, usually evil-smelling products, but such bacteria would not be found in any numbers in a well-maintained tank. If the marine tank is working well it would therefore be inadvisable to use an ultra-violet lamp. This equipment should only be used in cases where the water shows cloudiness due to bacteria.

Tank decoration

For a marine tank the decoration of the interior cannot be carried out in the same materials as are used in the freshwater aquarium. Many of the substances used for fresh water would tend

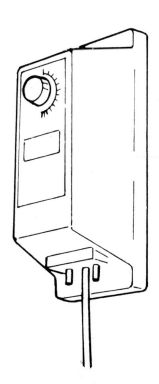

An ozonizer produces a mixture of ozone and air

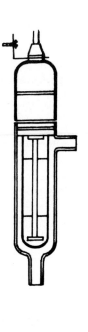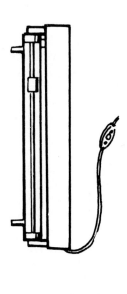

Two different kinds of ultraviolet lamp

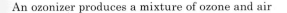

165

A 'living rock' from the Mediterranean

Sponges should be removed from rocks before they are transported, as they quickly die and foul the water

to lower the pH (e.g. roots, peat), instead of keeping it stable. On the other hand a sufficient amount of calcareous material, such as pieces of dead coral, will help to keep a stable pH. The horny elastic skeletons of the corals contain no calcium and so do not help to keep the water hard. They are only of use as additional items of decoration.

This is where one can use 'living rocks', which are pieces of sedimentary rock from the sea which have become encrusted with corals, dead and empty snail and bivalve shells, and disused calcareous worm tubes. All these items will have been bound together by calcareous algae and other organisms, producing a bizarre structure with numerous crevices and holes. On the reef itself such structures form the natural habitat for a rich fauna, consisting of sea-squirts, sponges, small tubeworms, free-living bristleworms, small crustaceans and tiny brittlestars. Pieces of 'living rock' from tropical seas would be very expensive, largely because of the cost of transport, but it is possible to find comparable pieces in subtropical areas, such as the Mediterranean Sea, in depths of 8–10 metres (c. 25–30

feet). If they are used, care should be taken to remove any sponges, as these die quickly and foul the water. Even if it contains no living animals, this type of calcareous material will keep the pH of the sea water constant, usually in the region of 8.0–8.3.

Pieces of dead coral are also much used in marine tanks, but they must be very carefully cleaned. Even when they are pure white and apparently clean, they may well harbour the remains of dead coral polyps. They should be placed in a plastic bucket and covered with a 5–10% solution of sodium hydroxide (caustic soda), care being taken to keep this dangerous material from any exposed parts of the body. After some days in this solution they can be removed and thoroughly washed in running water.

The substrate is also important, and is often a decorative feature. Ordinary sea sand can be used, but coral sand is even better, if it can be obtained. It comes from tropical seas and consists largely of broken fragments of coral. The shell gravel found in some temperate seas is a comparable material; it consists mainly of broken mollusc shells. When the tank contains

The sodium hydroxide used for cleaning coral skeletons is very caustic, so the coral should be placed in a plastic or enamel bucket (a), and the sodium hydroxide should be poured in from a similar bucket (b)

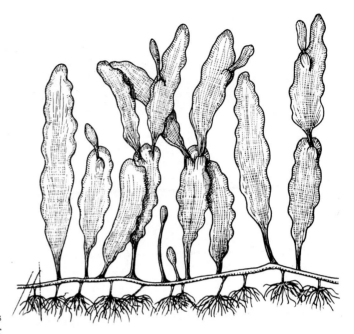

The green algae *Caulerpa prolifera* is the species that lives best in a marine aquarium

wrasses which like to bury themselves at night, at least part of the bottom should be covered with a soft substrate.

In general, the substrate need not be very thick, except perhaps when burrowing sea-anemones are being kept. A thin substrate may be disturbed by certain fishes, such as trigger-fishes and pufferfishes, in their search for something to eat. Coarse gravel is not suitable as a substrate because detritus accumulates between the individual pieces, and anaerobic, evil-smelling mud starts to form.

Marine algae

These plants are, generally speaking, not at all easy to keep in a marine tank. The ones that can be attempted are the green algae, provided there is an adequate oxygen supply and not too many fishes. Green algae usually thrive in tanks containing invertebrates, but they will be eaten by sea-urchins. Some of the green algae with leaf-like fronds are now being used very successfully. These belong to the genus *Caulerpa*, the best known species being *C. prolifera*, but others can

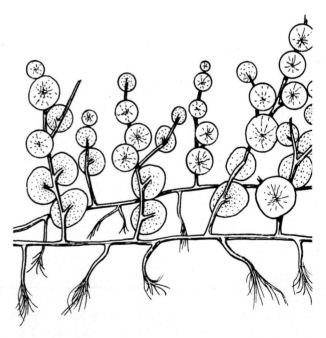

Caulerpa macrodisca

167

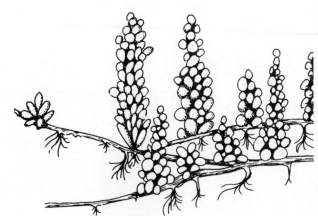

Caulerpa sertularioides

Caulerpa racemosa

be used, e.g. *C. macrodisca, C. racemosa* and *C. sertularioides*. These small algae spread by means of creeping stolons. In this way they may soon cover rocks and pieces of dead coral, provided they are not eaten by the fishes.

A newly established marine tank will rapidly acquire a growth of algae if there is sufficient light, and particularly if the tank has been 'inoculated' with a small amount of water from an older tank. These will usually be the microscopic algae known as diatoms, but they will continue to grow only if the water contains silicon compounds, which they use to make their external casing. Diatoms form a thin brown coating on rocks, but they will disappear quite quickly if the silicon supply is exhausted. Green algae with long, filamentous fronds can also be grown, but only if the fish population of the tank is fairly low, and the oxygen content of the water high.

Sea water

The quality of the water used in a marine tank is in every way as important as it is for a freshwater tank. In theory it is not too difficult to make up an artificial sea water from a mixture

of salts and trace elements. Salt mixtures in packs calculated for solution in different volumes of mains water are readily obtainable and easily dissolved.

The amounts given on the package will only give an approximate result. For greater precision one must find the density, using a hydrometer, which has a scale giving a direct reading. When salts are being dissolved to make artificial sea water, the whole solution should be left for several days, with a filter pump working, before the density is measured. The density reading will depend upon the temperature. The table opposite shows, for instance, that the density falls with increasing temperature.

On the average, tropical sea water at a temperature of 27°C (81°F) and with a density of 1.0220 (say 1.023) will have a salinity (salt content) of 35 parts per thousand. In fact, the salinity of sea water is remarkably close to this figure in all parts of the world, except in certain areas such as the Baltic Sea, where there is dilution by fresh water.

The solution of salts can, therefore, be brought up to a concentration that will give a density of 1.023 and this will suit most tropical marine fishes and invertebrates. In general, fishes will

Relationship between temperature, salinity and density of sea water

Temperature in °C										
20	1.0193	1.0200	1.0208	1.0215	1.0223	1.0231	1.0239	1.0246	1.0253	1.0259
21	1.0191	1.0198	1.0206	1.0214	1.0221	1.0229	1.0237	1.0244	1.0251	1.0258
22	1.0189	1.0197	1.0204	1.0212	1.0219	1.0227	1.0235	1.0242	1.0249	1.0256
23	1.0187	1.0195	1.0202	1.0210	1.0217	1.0224	1.0232	1.0240	1.0248	1.0254
24	1.0184	1.0193	1.0200	1.0207	1.0215	1.0222	1.0230	1.0238	1.0245	1.0252
25	1.0182	1.0190	1.0197	1.0205	1.0213	1.0220	1.0228	1.0235	1.0242	1.0250
26	1.0179	1.0187	1.0194	1.0202	1.0210	1.0217	1.0224	1.0232	1.0239	1.0247
27	1.0175	1.0184	1.0191	1.0199	1.0206	1.0213	1.0221	1.0229	1.0237	1.0243
28	1.0172	1.0180	1.0188	1.0195	1.0203	1.0210	1.0218	1.0225	1.0233	1.0240
29	1.0169	1.0176	1.0184	1.0192	1.0200	1.0207	1.0214	1.0221	1.0229	1.0237
30	1.0165	1.0172	1.0180	1.0188	1.0195	1.0202	1.0210	1.0217	1.0225	1.0233
Salinity in parts per thousand	28	29	30	31	32	33	34	35	36	37

tolerate higher salinities better than invertebrates, but there is no need for the water to have a salinity higher than 35 parts per thousand. If the salinity does increase owing to evaporation, it is a simple matter to reduce it by adding fresh water.

A further factor is that at higher salinities the capacity of the water to dissolve oxygen decreases. The following table shows how the oxygen saturation of the water depends upon temperature and density.

Oxygen in cc per litre

Temperature in °C	Density (approx.)	1.0225	1.0245	1.0255
10		6.54	6.46	6.37
15		5.94	5.87	5.80
20		5.44	5.38	5.31
25		4.99	4.94	4.85
30		4.56	4.50	4.44

The pH value

In natural sea water the pH is remarkably constant, at around 8.0–8.3. As a pH of 7.0 is neutral, it follows that sea water is slightly alkaline. The pH can be measured relatively simply, using a kit obtainable from aquarium dealers. This should be done at regular intervals, because in the enclosed environment of a tank the pH tends to fall, mainly because of the presence of dissolved carbonic acid. If the pH is found to be below 8.0 it can be adjusted by adding a small amount of sodium bicarbonate.

A newly established marine tank should be allowed to rest for some time before any fishes are introduced. This will allow the pH to become stabilized and the aerobic bacteria to break down toxic substances in the water. It will also allow the algae to settle in. If the tank is well lit and the water has been inoculated with some water from an established tank and is well aerated, then it should have become stabilized in three to four weeks, and be ready to receive the fishes.

Care of the fish

Feeding

As in the case of freshwater fishes, those in a marine tank should receive an adequate supply in sufficient variety, but not too much. In the wild, tropical marine fishes are accustomed to feeding throughout the day. They will do more or less the same in a well-maintained aquarium, for they will not only eat what they are given, but also some of the algae and the small invertebrates which live in among them. Shortly before darkness no more food should be put into the tank, because the fishes will mostly be preparing for their rest, and any unconsumed food will decompose overnight.

Variety in the diet is also an important factor. Most marine fishes will readily take the flesh of mussels or other available bivalve molluscs, but it may be some time before they will accept food to which they are unaccustomed. The introduction of various freeze-dried foods, such as mysids, shrimps and prawns has been a great help to the marine aquarist, for they can be kept for long periods, do not deteriorate, are easy to feed, and they have a high nutritive value. In addition, they avoid the necessity of using freshwater live foods, especially *Tubifex*, which die very rapidly in sea water, and if not consumed will very soon decompose and cause trouble. Deep-frozen foods are also suitable, although some, such as shrimps and prawns, may prove rather expensive. Less expensive foods, such as mussels, may only be obtainable at certain times of the year owing to difficulties of transport. In such cases it is a great advantage if the aquarist can deep-freeze them when they are available.

Diseases of coralfishes

Marine fishes, like those of fresh waters, also suffer from various diseases many of which have not been fully investigated. Perhaps the commonest of these is the parasitic infection by the protozoan *Oodinium ocellatum*. Many fishes are already carrying some infections when they are caught in the sea, but these may only develop and become serious under particularly unfavourable conditions. These include injury to the mucus epithelium during capture, cooling during transport, or the so-called oxygen shock caused by transfer from natural sea water saturated with oxygen, to water in a transport container which may have half the concentration of oxygen. Unsuitable feeding and the presence of toxic substances are also factors that may affect the development of a disease. Two types of disease may be recognized:
1. diseases caused by parasites
2. diseases due to certain external factors

Parasitic diseases are caused by organisms, such as protozoans (ciliates, flagellates, sporozoans), bacteria, viruses and fungi. The best known and most feared is the disease caused by the dinoflagellate protozoan *Oodinium ocellatum*. These microscopic parasites infect the skin of the fish where they grow ((a) in the adjoining figure). They then break loose as cysts and fall to the bottom. The cysts undergo a period of repeated divisions (b), which finally produce enormous numbers of free-swimming, flagellate dinospores (c), and these will attack a new host fish, and the cycle is repeated. In an aquarium tank, with much less water per fish than in the

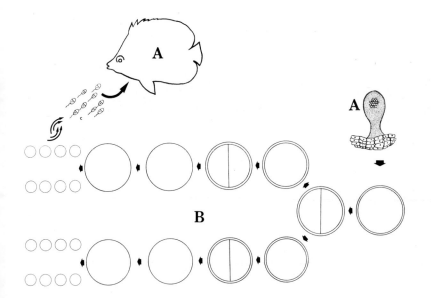

Life cycle of the parasitic marine dinoflagellate *Oodinium ocellatum*. The cysts on the fish's skin fall off and sink to the bottom. There the encysted parasite starts to divide (b), producing numerous motile spores (c), which then infect other fishes (a)

sea, the dinospores have no difficulty in finding and settling on a suitable host.

The multiplication of the parasites depends upon the temperature of the water. The parasites start to divide as soon as they have fallen from the host fish. At a temperature of over 25°C (77°F), each cyst will have produced 256 dinospores in three days. At lower temperatures the rate of multiplication is much slower, and below 10°C (50°F) it ceases altogether. If the fishes are removed from an infected tank the cycle will go on until the dinospore stage is reached. Then the dinospores, finding no available host, will all die quite quickly. Apart from high temperatures, in addition a slightly alkaline pH (around 8.0), a high content of nitrate, and a water density of 1.012 to 1.021 also stimulate multiplication of the parasites.

Various methods of treating *Oodinium* infections have been suggested. Some authorities have recommended the systematic transfer of the fishes through a series of tanks, the idea being to leave the parasites behind in tanks without fishes, so that they soon die off. Others have recommended treatment with various drugs such as mepacrine derivatives, but these should only be used by very experienced aquarists with full access to the specialist literature.

Perhaps the best method of controlling *Oodinium* is to treat the water with a solution of copper sulphate. This method was first published in

1955 by Robert P. Dempster in *Zoologica*, Vol. 40, pp. 133–139. Treatment must start as soon as symptoms of the disease have been observed; otherwise the parasites will multiply so rapidly in the warm water that all the fishes will become infected. There are various commercial preparations of copper sulphate on the market, but if necessary the solution can easily be prepared by a chemist or by the aquarist himself. The formula is 163 milligrams of copper sulphate to 100 litres of tank water. The best method of achieving the correct concentration is first to prepare a stock solution by dissolving 20 grams (c. $\frac{3}{4}$ oz) of copper sulphate in 5 litres (9 pints) of water. This solution should be kept in a well-stoppered plastic bottle. To use the chemical, add 25 cubic centimetres (millilitres), nearly 1 fluid oz, of the stock solution to every 100 litres (22 gallons) of aquarium water. The infected fishes can be left in this diluted copper solution for several days. During this period the concentration of copper may drop owing to its absorption onto rocks and other objects, and so some aquarists add a further dose of the copper sulphate stock solution. About half the previous amount has been suggested.

Treatment with copper sulphate or with certain other substances causes the fish to shed the mucus covering the body. This is a serious event in the life of a fish, and so treatment with copper sulphate should only be carried out on fishes

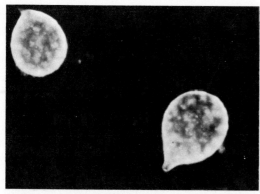

Individual parasites of *Oodinium ocellatum,*
x 250

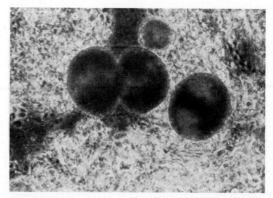

Oodinium ocellatum. Division of the parasite,
x 250

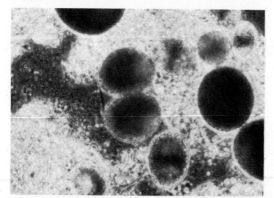

Oodinium ocellatum. Another photomicrograph
of the parasite dividing, x 250

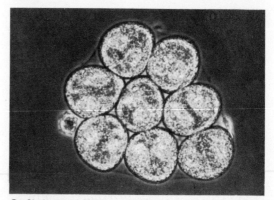

Oodinium ocellatum. A later stage of division,
x 420

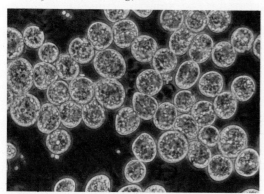

Oodinium ocellatum. The motile spores, x 650

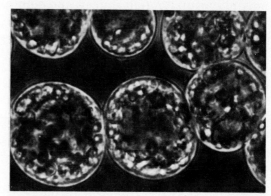

Oodinium ocellatum. The same spores, x 2000

that show the thin coating of tiny white spots
that is characteristic of *Oodinium.* Some zealous
aquarists use the copper treatment as a preventive on fishes that are apparently healthy, but
this is not to be recommended.

It is, of course, quite essential that the presence of *Oodinium* should be correctly diagnosed before treatment. As in the case of white
spot *(Ichthyophthirius)* in the freshwater aqua-

rium, the first sign of *Oodinium* is the appearance
of tiny white spots or nodules on the skin of the
fish. These are often particularly noticeable on
transparent fins. If the infection is not treated it
will soon cover the whole fish, which will appear
as though powdered. In the next stage the gills
become infected, and the fish will show respiratory distress and will remain just below the
water surface or close to a source of oxygen. If

the infection has reached this stage the fish can scarcely be saved.

As a preventive measure against *Oodinium*, every opportunity should be taken of reducing the content of nitrate in the water. This can be done by removing detritus and any scraps of unconsumed food from the bottom, and also by ensuring that there are no decaying fragments of algae at the water surface. A high nitrate content can also be reduced by changing a proportion of the water at intervals.

Under no circumstances should copper treatment be used in a tank containing invertebrates. The presence of this metal is lethal to such animals, and the rapid decomposition of their bodies will soon kill off the other inmates of the tank. Filamentous green algae are also adversely affected by copper. Certain fish species, such as the butterflyfishes of the family Chaetodontidae, do not tolerate a high dosage of copper, and in such cases the dosage recommended above should be reduced by 20–30%. If the tank is fitted with a foam filter, it should be turned off during the period of treatment; otherwise the drug will be removed from the tank water. On the other hand, there should be full aeration and water circulation.

Cryptocarion disease

This is caused by a ciliate protozoan, *Cryptocarion irritans*, which settles under the fish's skin. It appears as white nodules on the fins, skin and eyes and is very infectious. With a slight infection the fishes start to rub themselves against the tank decoration, with the result that the nodules spread over the whole of the body, and inflamed areas of skin start to fall off. This disease can be treated in the same way as *Oodinium*, but here, too, great care must be taken to ensure that the treatment is not stopped before the last nodules have disappeared.

Fungal infections

These can be recognized as opaque coatings on the body and fins. The terms fin rot, mouth rot and others have been applied to different forms of fungal infection. The causative agents are various kinds of aquatic fungi, which are probably present in most waters but only become pathogenic and settle on fishes when environmental conditions change. Fishes from the Caribbean area appear to be more susceptible to fungal infection than those from other seas. In many cases of fungal infection a change of the tank water may help. When only the fins are attacked it is possible to snip off the affected areas, taking care not to damage the fin bases. In particularly serious cases of fungal infection the fishes can be treated for some days in a tank containing 25 milligrams of the fungicide griseofulvin per litre of water.

Lymphocystis

This is a less infectious disease caused by a virus which, under unfavourable aquarium conditions, penetrates the cells of a fish and causes them to swell. It can be recognized by the pearly nodules of varying sizes, particularly on the back and the dorsal fins. It is usually possible to cure this disease by proper care of the fish, without recourse to treatment by any drug. In most cases the nodules appear first on the fins, and it is then possible to cut off the infected areas carefully with a pair of fine scissors. In particularly bad cases the fishes can be given a copper sulphate bath (as for *Oodinium*) over a period, or they can be kept in a potassium iodide bath. Here the stock solution is made up by dissolving 5 grams (c. $\frac{1}{8}$ oz) of iodine and 500 grams (c. 18 oz) of potassium iodide in 5 litres (c. 1.1 gallons) of distilled water. The dosage is the same as for copper, i.e. 25 cc (nearly 1 fluid oz) of stock solution for each 100 litres (22 gallons) of tank water.

Swimbladder trouble

Sometimes one sees fishes that are swimming jerkily in an oblique position, usually with head upwards. This is an abnormal symptom caused by inflammation of the swimbladder. It is usually the result of a drop in temperature during transport. The fishes should be put into a separate tank with a high water temperature (28–30°C or 82–86°F). If the fishes are feeding they can be given an antibiotic in the food. For instance, mussel flesh soaked in aureomycin will help to reinforce the heat treatment. There are other diseases affecting marine fishes which are described in specialist literature.

Marine fishes

Several factors have to be taken into consideration in deciding on the fish species to keep in a marine tank. Coloration is obviously important, but size, fin shape and swimming methods are also of interest. Apart from these more aesthetic considerations, care must be taken to ensure that large, clumsy forms, such as triggerfishes, are not put into a tank with more delicate species which will have their fins nipped.

Fishes and invertebrates can, of course, be kept in the same tank, but this needs considerable care and experience. Obviously it would be unwise to put into a tank with invertebrates any fishes that will eat them. Such fishes include butterflyfishes, sweetlips, larger wrasse, parrot-fishes, triggerfishes, filefishes, boxfishes, porcupinefishes and pufferfishes. Fishes that are suitable include smaller marine angelfishes and surgeonfishes, as well as various groupers, small gobies, blennies and scorpionfishes. The much discussed association between sea-anemones and clownfishes of the genus *Amphiprion* is only successful in the confines of a tank if the anemone is considerably larger than the fishes. If the fishes are too large they jostle the mouth region of the anemone too much, and it eventually shrinks and dies. There are so many marine fishes that it will be worthwhile in the following pages to give some details on a representative selection of those that are available.

Some features of fish fins:
D = dorsal fin (the signs D 1 and D 2 are only used when
the dorsal fin is in two parts)
C = caudal fin   P = pectoral fins
A = anal fin   h = hard or spiny rays
V = ventral fins   w = soft or segmented rays

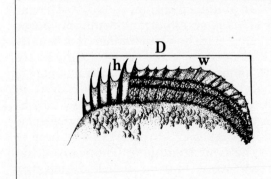

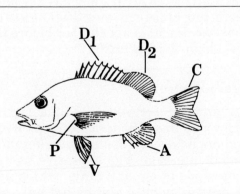

Moray-eels

Many of these are very large and therefore only suitable for the public aquarium, but there are several species which can be kept in a home aquarium, at any rate when they are young. One of these is the blue ribbon eel *Rhinomuraena ambonensis*, a slender fish up to 120 cm (48 in) long with fantastic blue and yellow coloration. Others that have a rather stouter body include the zebra moray *Echidna zebra* (up to 120 cm or 48 in), the snowflake moray *E. nebulosa* (80 cm or 32 in) and the voracious leopard moray *Gymnothorax favagineus* (= *G. tesselata*) (150 cm or 60 in). Moray-eels spend the day in hiding and become active as soon as it starts to get dark. They require a spacious tank and should not be kept together with smaller fishes. The tank should have a close-fitting lid as these are inquisitive fishes which often manage to squeeze through quite small apertures. Once they have settled in, moray-eels are not difficult to feed, and will readily take chopped fish and squid, as well as mussel flesh.

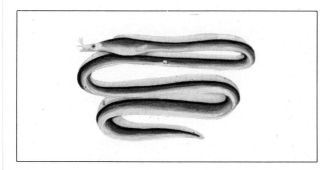

Rhinomuraena ambonensis

Plotosus lineatus

In the sea many of the moray-eels live in fairly shallow water, often among rocks or in places where there are small cavities. Some of them apparently live gregariously.

In tropical and subtropical waters many of the larger moray-eels feed primarily on octopus, which they seize with their sharp-pointed teeth. A moray cannot cut the prey into pieces with these teeth. Instead they have been observed to twist their body round very rapidly on its own axis so that the prey is broken into pieces.

Marine catfishes

These are nocturnal fishes, not often seen in the home aquarium. Great care must be taken in handling them, as the dorsal and pectoral fins have poison spines. Like their relatives in fresh water, these catfishes are often useful as scavengers. They are best bought when quite young, and kept in a small shoal.

There are several species in the seas off eastern Africa and south-east Asia extending to Japan, the Philippines and northern Australia, and sometimes moving into brackish waters, or even into rivers. The species most commonly available is *Plotosus lineatus*, which grows to a length of 70 cm (27 in).

This species has an elongated, torpedo-like body and a large head, with four pairs of characteristic short barbels. The first dorsal fin is normal, but the second dorsal fin is combined with the caudal and anal fins to form a single fringe, which may have a dark edge. They can be kept in sea or brackish water, preferably at a temperature of 22–26°C (72–79°F).

Anglerfishes

These bizarre fishes are characterized by the 'angle' or lure, a modified first dorsal fin ray positioned between the mouth and eyes, which has a flap of skin at the end. The larger species are of course quite unsuitable for the aquarium, but there are a few quite small species which show amazingly good camouflage. One of these is the Sargassum fish *Histrio histrio*, which grows to a length of 15 cm (6 in). In nature this species feeds exclusively on live food, so it is not easy to keep in the aquarium.

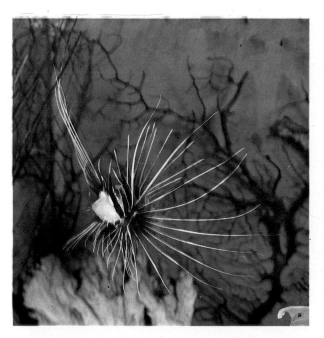

Pterois radiata

Pterois volitans

Scorpionfishes

These bizarre fishes with much-developed filmy fins may appear at first sight to be rather delicate, fragile creatures, but they are in fact voracious predators, and the dorsal and pectoral fin rays are highly venomous. They approach their prey by more or less floating towards it, scarcely moving the fins. When close enough the very large mouth opens, and the prey is engulfed and swallowed. In the aquarium they can be accustomed to taking pieces of fish or even mammalian heart, but they prefer live fishes. They will, however, pay no attention to pieces that have dropped to the bottom of the tank. The genus *Pterois* contains the dragonfishes, also known as lionfishes and turkeyfishes. The species most commonly imported are *P. volitans*, *P. radiata*, *P. lunulata* and *P. antennata* which reach lengths of up to 25 cm (c. 10 in). Smaller relatives sometimes available are *Dendrochirus brachypterus* (15 cm or 6 in) and *D. zebra*.

Pterois volitans

Pterois lunulata

Synanceja verrucosa

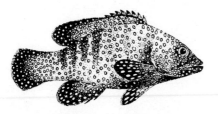

Epinephelus (Cephalopholis) argus

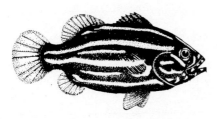

Grammistes sexlineatus

Stonefishes

These are neither beautiful nor decorative, nor active, nor in any way worth their cost to the average aquarist. The dorsal and pectoral fin rays are extremely venomous, far more so than those of the dragonfishes. During the day stonefishes lie on the bottom and are so well camouflaged that they look like stones covered with a growth of algae. They will eat almost anything, but particularly other fishes, including those that are as large as themselves, so they should on no account be put into a tank with other fishes. Two species of these highly dangerous fishes sometimes imported are *Synanceja verrucosa* and *S. horrida*.

Groupers

The groupers of the family Serranidae are active predators which hide away in caves or under rock ledges, ready to dash out and seize passing prey, a task for which the large mouth is well adapted. Groupers do not grow very rapidly, so smaller specimens can be kept for quite a time. They will soon feed on pieces of chopped fish or squid.

Although many of the groupers are large, there are several small tropical species which are very attractively marked. Of the species imported one of the best known is the black grouper *Epinephelus (Cephalopholis) argus* (38 cm or 15 in), which has a beautiful spotted pattern. Others include *E.(C.) miniatus* (46 cm or 18 in) and various *Epinephelus* species of the subgenus *Epinephelus*.

The six-lined grouper *Grammistes sexlineatus* (25 cm or $9\frac{3}{4}$ in) sometimes classified in a separate family, has proved a fairly hardy aquarium fish that is easy to keep. It comes from the Indo-Pacific and is certainly voracious, so it should only be kept with other fishes that are considerably larger than itself.

The family Grammidae

These are more peaceful fishes, and they are not predatory. The species known to aquarists is the royal gramma *Gramma loreto* from the Caribbean Sea and Bermuda, which reaches a length of 6–8 cm ($2\frac{1}{4}$–3 in). These fishes live in the coral reefs and are evidently rather difficult to catch,

Gramma loreto

and this may account for their high price. In the aquarium they tend to live in the more sheltered places, and it is sometimes difficult to get them established in captivity.

Cardinal fishes

The dominant colour of these fishes (family Apogonidae) is red. Like the similarly coloured soldierfishes they are nocturnal or crepuscular in their habits. They are quite small, seldom reaching a length of about 10 cm (3¾ in), and they

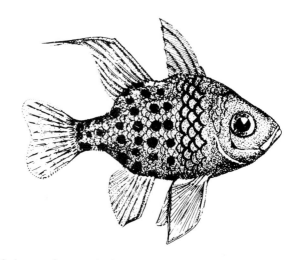

Sphaeramia nematoptera

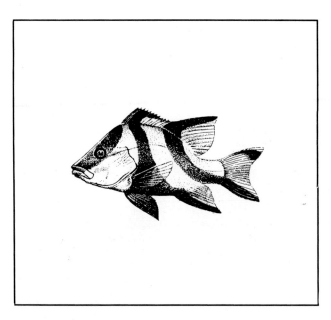

Lutjanus sebae

have the dorsal fin divided into two parts. Some, if not all, of the species are known to be mouth-brooders, and apparently in most cases it is the male who incubates the eggs in his mouth.

The commonly imported pyjama cardinal fish *Sphaeramia nematoptera* (8 cm or 3 in) usually does well in the aquarium, but it must be kept in a small shoal, as solitary specimens do not survive. The shoal will remain more or less inactive during the day, but start to move around as soon as the light fades.

Snappers

The snappers of the family Lutjanidae are highly esteemed as edible fishes in the tropical and subtropical areas where they occur. They are rather aggressive predators that grow rapidly, and they soon become too large for most home aquarium tanks. The species imported include the blue-striped snapper *Lutjanus kasmira* (38 cm or 15 in) and particularly *L. sebae*, about the same size, which is brightly coloured when young, but becomes much duller with increasing age.

Sweetlips

Gaterin (= Plectorinchus) orientalis, juvenile pattern above, adult pattern below

These fishes belong to the family Pomadasyidae. They do quite well in the aquarium, and they live and feed mainly on the bottom of the tank. The species most commonly kept in the aquarium is the oriental sweetlips *Gaterin (= Plectorinchus) orientalis*, but others appear on the market from time to time. The young fishes are perhaps more attractive than the adults, which change colour with increasing age.

Fingerfishes (family Monodactylidae)

Most aquarists know these as brackish-water fishes. In fact the young occur in fresh and brackish waters, but they tend to move towards the sea as they grow older. Two species are widely available: *Monodactylus argenteus*, the mono or fingerfish (23 cm or 9 in) from the Indian Ocean, and *M. sebae* (20 cm or 7¾ in), a rather taller species fish from the west coast of Africa. They feed well in the aquarium, and as they get older should be kept only in sea water.

Monodactylus argenteus

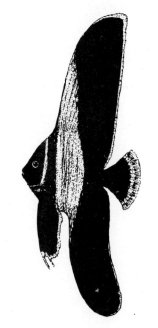

Platax pinnatus

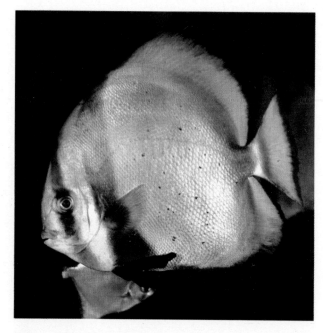

Platax orbicularis, adult

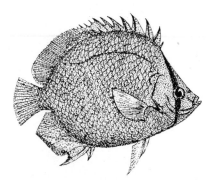

Chaetodon citrinellus

Chaetodon fremblii

Batfishes (family Ephippidae)

Three species are available from dealers, namely *Platax orbicularis* and *P. teira*, which under good conditions may grow to a length of 50–60 cm (20–23 in) and the rather smaller *P. pinnatus*. They come from coastal waters in the Indo-Pacific region. In the aquarium the period of acclimatization is sometimes difficult, but after this batfishes usually do well, although the coloration tends to become paler with age.

Butterflyfishes (family Chaetodontidae)

This is a large family with numerous species which live, usually in pairs, in and around tropical coral reefs. Most of them are 15–20 cm (6–8 in) long. They spend the day searching for food, mainly small invertebrates, which they pick out of crevices in the corals with the elongated, often pointed mouth. They should not be kept with invertebrates such as prawns, which have long appendages, as they tend to bite pieces off. When buying butterflyfishes care should be taken to ensure that they are feeding properly.

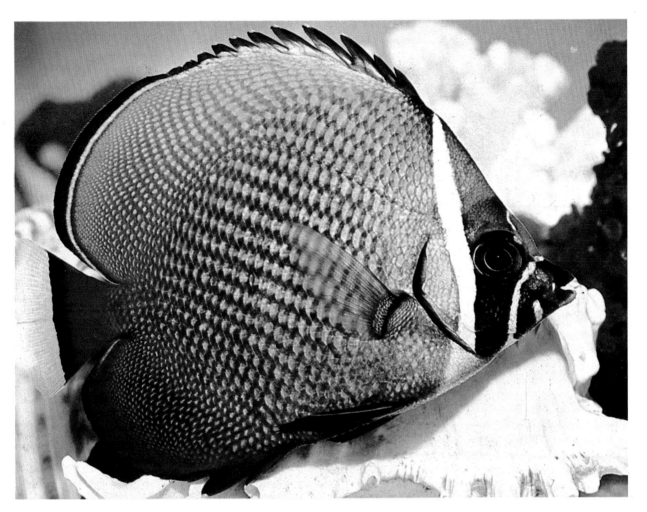

Chaetodon collaris

Chelmon rostratus

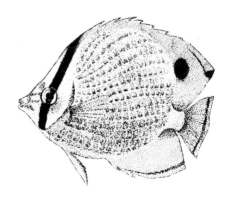

Chaetodon ocellatus

above: *Chaetodon semilarvatus*

below: *Chaetodon tinkeri* (left) and *Centropyge bicolor* (right)

Hemitaurichthys polylepis

They are often aggressive towards members of their own species, but not usually towards other species. They are very susceptible to *Oodinium* infections, and unfortunately they do not tolerate the usual copper sulphate treatment very well.

Over the years several species have been imported, and of these some of the best are *Chaetodon collaris, C. semilarvatus, C. auriga, C. citrinellus, C. fremblii* and *C. ocellatus*. The more recently introduced *C. quadrimaculatus* and *C. tinkeri* are still expensive. The family also includes species with long snouts, such as *Chelmon rostratus* and *Forcipiger flavissimus*, which are well adapted for extracting food from long, narrow crevices in the corals.

Chaetodon quadrimaculatus

Marine angelfishes (family Pomacanthidae)

The members of this family have one point in common, namely that they are all quite brilliantly coloured, and in this respect can stand comparison with the most brightly coloured birds and butterflies. In most of the species the coloration and pattern of the juvenile fishes are quite different from those of the adults. This is probably correlated with the extreme territorial behaviour of marine angelfishes. Adults of a species often fight bitterly with one another, and it is probable that the possession of a completely different pattern and colour will protect the young from the attacks of their elders. Most species are imported with a juvenile pattern, often of blue and white stripes, but even at this stage the different species can be recognized by certain distinctive features in the pattern.

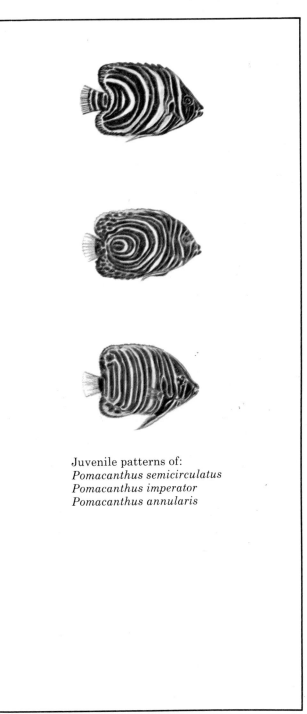

Juvenile patterns of:
Pomacanthus semicirculatus
Pomacanthus imperator
Pomacanthus annularis

Pomacanthus semicirculatus

Marine angelfishes swim about very peacefully, except during territorial fighting, and often hold themselves in an oblique position with the dorsal fin towards the aquarium glass. Pomacanthids should feed readily on chopped fish or squid, but they must be given some plant food, such as large lettuce leaves, unless the tank has a sufficient growth of algae. Nevertheless, some are difficult to feed, and present prob-

lems. These include the royal empress angelfish *Pygoplites diacanthus* (20 cm or 7¾ in) from the Indo-Pacific. This is one of the most attractive of all coral fishes, but only suitable for the very advanced marine aquarist.

The marine angelfishes from the Caribbean area include a few wonderful fishes, such as the queen angelfish *Holacanthus ciliaris* (60 cm or 24 in) and the blue angelfish *H. isabelita* (46 cm or 18 in), but these are unfortunately not often available to the aquarist. The more commonly imported species from this part of the world include *Pomacanthus paru* and *P. arcuatus*. These usually settle down well in the aquarium and grow rapidly. Their maximum length is about 40 cm ($15\frac{3}{4}$ in). The rather smaller rock beauty *Holacanthus tricolor* (30 cm or 12 in) and the cherubfish *Centropyge argi* (6 cm or $2\frac{1}{4}$ in) are also imported from time to time.

Pygoplites diacanthus

below: *Holacanthus ciliaris* adult, with a juvenile showing vertical bars (right)

Holacanthus arcuatus

Arusetta asfur

Centropyge loriculus

The Hawaiian Islands also yield some of the smaller pomacanthids such as the black-banded angelfish *Holacanthus arcuatus* (18 cm or 7 in) and the very attractive but expensive *Centropyge loriculus*. However, the main area for pomacanthids is undoubtedly the Indo-Pacific, a vast area extending from the Red Sea and East Africa to the East Indies and eastwards to Queensland, Fiji and many of the island groups of the South Pacific. Some of the species from this area grow quite large and they include *Pygoplites diacanthus* (20 cm or $7\frac{3}{4}$ in), the imperial angelfish *Pomacanthus imperator* (36 cm or 14 in), *P. semicirculatus* (40 cm or $15\frac{3}{4}$ in) and *Arusetta asfur* (14 cm or $5\frac{1}{2}$ in). Other species from the Indo-Pacific are the blue king angelfish *Pomacanthus annularis* (40 cm or $15\frac{3}{4}$ in), the blue-girdled angelfish *Euxiphipops navarchus* (30 cm or $11\frac{3}{4}$ in), the six-barred angelfish *E. sexstriatus* and the yellow-faced angelfish *E. xanthometopon* (30 cm or $11\frac{3}{4}$ in), as well as a great number of species of *Holacanthus* (e.g. the three-spot angelfish, *H. trimaculatus*) and of *Centropyge* (e.g. *C. flavissimus* and *C. heraldi*). The whole family is obviously one that is highly attractive to the marine aquarist, but the various species are still rather difficult to keep for any length of time, except in the hands of the really experienced.

Pomacanthus annularis, with a moray-eel (below)

Euxiphipops sexstriatus

Euxiphipops navarchus

Euxiphipops xanthometopon

Damselfishes and anemone-fishes

The family Pomacentridae contains several fishes suitable for the marine aquarium. Most of these are quite small, and they live in shoals near to the coral stocks, or in some cases in close association with sea-anemones. In spite of their small size pomacentrids tend to be aggressive, and on this account many aquarists find them unsatisfactory. Nevertheless, some of them are very attractive.

The damselfishes include *Abudefduf oxyodon* (11 cm or $4\frac{1}{4}$ in), *A. xanthurus*, and the rather larger sergeant-major *A. saxatilis*. In the genus *Dascyllus*, the domino damselfish *D. trimaculatus* (12 cm or $4\frac{3}{4}$ in) is very commonly imported, and its black-and-white pattern provides a good contrast to the brilliant colours of some of its relatives. Other members of this genus include *D. aruanus* (9 cm or $3\frac{1}{2}$ in) and *D. reticulatus* (7 cm or $2\frac{3}{4}$ in). Several of the species have a bright yellow tail, as for instance *Pomacentrus melanochir* (7 cm or $2\frac{3}{4}$ in), but some of these are difficult to name. Confusion is also caused by the fact that several of the damselfishes show brilliant colours when young but lose these with increasing age.

Anemone-fishes are so called because they live in close association with certain large tropical sea-anemones, swimming in and out of the tentacles; a behaviour pattern that would be fatal to other fishes. Anemone-fishes, mostly in

Dascyllus aruanus

Abudefduf saxatilis

Abudefduf oxyodon

Dascyllus reticulatus

Abudefduf xanthurus

Dascyllus aruanus

Dascyllus trimaculatus

Abudefduf oxyodon

below left: *Amphiprion ocellaris*
below right: *Abudefduf cyaneus*

Amphiprion sebae

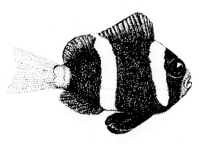

Amphiprion clarkii

Amphiprion biaculeatus

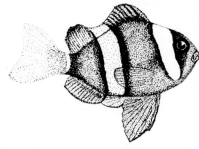

Amphiprion sebae

Amphiprion polymnus

the genus *Amphiprion*, all come from the Indo-Pacific area. They can be kept together with their anemone in a marine tank, and in many cases the two partners live together for quite a time. There is, however, a tendency to keep large specimens of the fish with an anemone that is too small. It seems that the fish may hinder food intake by the anemone, which eventually dies.

There has been a certain amount of confusion in the naming of *Amphiprion* species, partly because some of the species resemble each other very closely when young, and partly because their coloration changes with age. At any rate, the nomenclature of the genus has been revised, with the result that aquarists and dealers now have to learn and use a new set of names. Thus, the common anemone-fish or clownfish *Amphiprion ocellaris* (10 cm or $3\frac{3}{4}$ in) was formerly *A. percula*. Other species imported include *A. sebae* and *A. polymnus* (12 cm or $4\frac{3}{4}$ in), but the most satisfactory from the aquarium viewpoint appears to be *A. ephippium* (15 cm or 6 in). This is possibly because it does not depend so much as the other species on the presence of a sea-anemone.

Wrasses

The wrasses belong to the large family Labridae, which has a great number of species in tropical and subtropical waters, but there are also some in temperate waters. Wrasses are popular aquarium fishes and several species are available on the market. However, before buying, it is best to find out how large the chosen fishes will grow, as some species would soon outgrow the average tank. They feed well on almost any food, live or dead, and do not appear to be too demanding as regards the quality of the water.

In recent years the cleaner wrasse *Labroides dimidiatus* (10 cm or $3\frac{3}{4}$ in) has become one of the most popular of all marine aquarium fishes. This is not because of its beauty, although it is quite attractive, but because of its habit of removing parasites and loose fragments of skin from other fishes, a task which the latter obviously encourage, and they never attack the little wrasse. The quite unrelated false cleaner *Aspidontus taeniatus*, a blenny, has evolved a pattern that is strikingly like that of the cleaner wrasse, but it is an aggressive fish that bites the fins of other species.

The genus *Thalassoma* provides several excellent fast-growing aquarium fishes. These include the blue-head *T. bifasciatum* (5 cm or 6 in) from the Caribbean Sea and the green or lyretail wrasse, *T. lunare* (25 cm or $9\frac{3}{4}$ in) from the Indo-Pacific. Some wrasses change their coloration as they grow older. One of the most striking instances is *Coris gaimardi (=formosa)*, which comes from the Indo-Pacific. When young this species is red with a white pattern, but adults are completely different in colour (see illustrations below).

Cleaner wrasse, *Labroides dimidiatus*

False cleaner, *Aspidontus taeniatus*

Another cleaner wrasse, *Labroides quadrilineatus*, from the Red Sea

below: *Coris gaimardi*, adult, with a juvenile (small picture) for comparison

Parrotfishes

These fishes of the family Scaridae are not really suitable for the home aquarium, partly because they are rather large, but mainly because they have specialized feeding habits. The mouth is in the form of a strong beak, hence the popular name, and it is used to bite off and chew pieces of coral and other calcareous structures. This is scarcely a habit that would be popular in most aquarium tanks.

Blennies

This is a widespread family, the Blenniidae, with numerous species in tropical, subtropical and temperate seas. The false cleaner *Aspidontus taeniatus*, already mentioned under wrasses,

belongs in this family. During recent years several attractive blennies have been imported from the tropics. These are all small fishes with a characteristic bull-like head. Two species of *Meiacanthus*, namely the forktail blenny *M.*

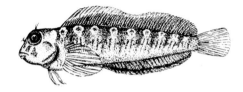

Blennius sp.

Synchiropus splendidus

atrodorsalis and the yellow-tailed blenny *M. mossambicus* have proved successful for the aquarium. Some of the subtropical species, such as *Blennius pavo* (12 cm or $4\frac{3}{4}$ in) and *B. sphinx* (8 cm or 3 in), both from the Mediterranean Sea, have proved very hardy, if somewhat quarrelsome, aquarium fishes.

Synchiropus

These fishes of the dragonet family (Callionymidae) have only recently been seen in the aquarium. The species most commonly kept is the mandarin fish *Synchiropus splendidus* from Indonesian waters, which scarcely exceeds a length of 12 cm ($4\frac{3}{4}$ in) in a marine tank. The sexes are easy to distinguish for in the male the front rays of the first dorsal fin are much elongated. These fishes require a tank that has been established over a long period, and has a rich growth of algae. They feed primarily on the small invertebrates that live among the algae, taking them with the slightly protrusible mouth. They cannot really be kept for any length of time on a diet of *Tubifex* and *Artemia*. The tank should not be too small, for males will fight unless they have plenty of space.

A less brilliantly coloured species, *S. ocellatus*, is also available from time to time, and it is rather smaller than *S. splendidus*. It has a very handsome tall dorsal fin which is beautifully coloured.

Gobies

The gobies form a very large family, the Gobiidae, with at least 600 species. They are mainly small fishes, and many of them do well in the aquarium. Some spend the greater part of the day lying on a rock or on a coral stock, while others are active, elegant swimmers. Newly introduced gobies tend to be shy and to spend their time hidden away in a corner of the tank, but they gradually start to come out. They will eat almost anything, and since they have a large mouth can take relatively large morsels.

For a marine tank the best known species are the neon goby *Gobiosoma oceanops* (6 cm or $2\frac{1}{4}$ in), which comes from the Caribbean area; the slightly smaller *Gobiodon citrinus* from the Indo-Pacific and Red Sea, and the larger scissor-tail goby *Ptereleotris tricolor* (14 cm or $5\frac{1}{2}$ in) also from the Indo-Pacific area.

Surgeonfishes

This is an attractive family of marine fishes, known as the Acanthuridae, many of which can be kept in marine tanks. Their popular name refers to the small sharp spine on each side of the caudal peduncle. This 'scalpel' is movable and can be folded back or erected so that it stands out at right angles to the body. In the latter position it forms a dangerous weapon for attack or defence. In the aquarium, surgeonfishes can be seen to use this spine when fighting other members of their own species or other fishes that threaten them. On this account many aquarists prefer to keep a single surgeonfish in a

Zebrasoma flavescens

Gobiosoma oceanops

Zebrasoma desjardini

tank on its own, to prevent rivals from having their flanks ripped open.

Many species of surgeonfish appear on the market, and these include such brilliantly coloured species as the white-breasted surgeonfish *Acanthurus leucosternon* (30 cm or $11\frac{3}{4}$ in) from the Indian Ocean, and other species in the same genus, e.g. the smaller golden-rimmed sur-geonfish *A. glaucopareius* from the Philippines, and the clown surgeon *A. lineatus* (18 cm or 7 in) from the Indo-Pacific area. Another good species is the blue surgeon *Paracanthurus hepatus* (30 cm or $11\frac{3}{4}$ in) also from the Indo-Pacific. The genus *Zebrasoma* is also represented in marine tanks by several interesting species which tend to be quite aggressive. These include

Acanthurus leucosternon

the sailfin tang *Z. veliferum* (40 cm or 15¾ in) from the Indo-Pacific, and the rather more peaceful yellow tang *Z. flavescens* from the Hawaiian area. The yellow-tailed *Z. xanthurum* (40 cm or 15¾ in) from the Indo-Pacific and Red Sea is another fine species, but specimens on the market are almost always too large for the home aquarium, although they make excellent exhibits in a public aquarium. The form known as *Z. desjardini* is very similar in external appearance to *Z. veliferum*, but its tail is marked with numerous spots which are lacking in the latter species.

Species in the genus *Naso* do not have the single scalpel on each side of the caudal peduncle, but instead a couple of spines which are not movable. They use these for defence. Some, but not all, of the *Naso* species have a hornlike projection on the forehead which increases in size with age. Species with the horn include *N. brevirostris* (43 cm or 17 in) and *N. unicornis* (56 cm or 22 in). As in the case of many surgeonfishes it is sometimes difficult to get the *Naso* species to take aquarium food. At the start they should be offered plenty of lettuce leaves, and these often bridge the gap until the fishes begin to take mussel flesh.

Paracanthurus hepatus

201

Zanclus canescens

Moorish idols

This is a small group of rather strange, quite small, marine fishes which form the family Zanclidae. To most aquarists these are problem fishes, but this is largely because they inadvertently buy slightly damaged individuals. Moorish idols require a large tank with a volume of at least 350 litres (c. 75 gallons). Like the surgeonfishes they need plenty of plant food, so a good growth of algae in the tank will be an advantage. At one time Moorish idols were classified as several different species, based on small differences in pattern and so on, but this is unnecessary and it is best to use the single scientific name *Zanclus canescens* (20 cm or 7¾ in).

Rabbitfishes or Spinefeet

These are fishes of the tropical Indo-Pacific, forming the family Siganidae, and they feed

Siganus (Lo) vulpinus

mainly on plant food. Many of them have become popular aquarium fishes. The long spiny rays of the dorsal fin can be erected when the fish is threatened, and these can give nasty wounds to the unwary aquarist who puts his hand in the tank. It has been said that there is venom associated with the spines.

The best known member of the family is *Siganus (Lo) vulpinus* (23 cm or 9 in), which has a yellow body and a black-and-white striped head with a long, trumpet-like mouth. This species, which comes from the Indo-Pacific, often does very well in a marine tank, and can be kept together with other fishes. Other species suitable for the marine aquarium are *Siganus vermiculatus* (38 cm or 15 in) and *S. virgatus* (26 cm or 10¼ in).

Triggerfishes and filefishes

The strangely shaped triggerfishes of the family Balistidae are often beautifully coloured, and all have a very large head which occupies up to a third of the body length. The mouth, on the other hand, is quite small, but it is equipped with powerful teeth. The first dorsal fin ray is in the form of a large spine which can be erected and locked into position by the second shorter spiny ray, forming a trigger mechanism. The erectile spine serves as a weapon and also helps to anchor or wedge the fishes in rocky crevices during the night. Although underwater films often show groups of triggerfishes swimming more or less together off the coral reefs, these fishes are best kept separate in the aquarium. Small specimens can be kept for a time in a community tank but the day comes when they become aggressive and have to be separated.

In their natural environment triggerfishes feed mainly on marine invertebrates, such as crustaceans, sea-urchins and bivalve molluscs, and so can at any rate be given mussel flesh in the aquarium. Larger specimens will eat lean heart or liver, chopped into pieces to suit the fish's mouth.

Species that are frequently kept in the aquarium include the undulate triggerfish *Balistapus undulatus* (30 cm or 11¾ in), the clown triggerfish *Balistoides niger* (50 cm or 19½ in), the black triggerfish *Odonus niger* (50 cm or 19½ in), the similarly sized blue-lined triggerfish

Pseudobalistes fuscus

Pseudobalistes fuscus all from the Indo-Pacific area, and the very bizarre Picasso triggerfish *Rhinecanthus aculeatus* (33 cm or 13 in) which lives off the coasts of Hawaii.

Filefishes of the family Monacanthidae are also sometimes kept, and some do well in the aquarium. One species, the long-nosed filefish *Oxymonacanthus longirostris* (10 cm or 3¾ in), with beautiful orange and green coloration, is rather a food specialist, for in its natural home on the reefs in the Indo-Pacific it feeds mainly on coral polyps. This species has to be kept in a

Balistoides niger

Rhinecanthus aculeatus

Odonus niger

small shoal, but it is one of the most difficult of all marine fishes, and it cannot be recommended to any but the most experienced aquarists. The tasseled filefish *Monacanthus spinosissimus* is said to be relatively easy to keep.

Boxfishes

These fishes mostly have an angular box-like body, so the popular name is apt. Scientifically they form the family Ostraciontidae. The body is enclosed in bony plates, except for the fins. The tail fin is attached by a particularly flexible peduncle, and it acts as a rudder. The mouth is small, but with powerful teeth adapted for seizing and crushing hard-shelled animals, particularly crustaceans.

These are not easy fishes to keep in the aquarium and they often do not survive the period of acclimatization. It is a good idea to keep several individuals (even of different species) together, as they appear to learn from each other to take the substitute foods offered by the aquarist. Dying boxfishes produce a poisonous substance which may kill other perfectly healthy fishes.

Species that are kept in marine tanks include the long-horned cowfish *Lactoria cornuta* (50 cm or 19½ in), the spotted boxfish *Ostracion meleagris* (= *lentiginosum*) (20 cm or 7¾ in), and the thornback boxfish *Tetrosomus gibbosus* (30 cm or 11¾ in), all from the Indo-Pacific area.

Pufferfishes

This family, the Tetraodontidae, has numerous representatives in all tropical and subtropical seas, and there are also some species in fresh and brackish waters. The more or less ovoid body is covered by particularly tough skin. Pufferfishes are capable of inflating the body, hence the popular name, and their flesh which is eaten in Japan, for instance, is often poisonous. The mouth is small with the teeth fused to form a powerful beak which is well adapted for crushing hard-shelled invertebrates. Pufferfishes can sometimes be seen to blow away the sand with a jet of water in order to expose crustaceans and other suitable prey. At feeding time in an aquarium they often come to the surface and puff a jet of water at the aquarist as he lifts the tank cover. They are usually not difficult to feed on

Lactoria cornuta

Ostracion meleagris

Canthigaster valentini

Porcupinefishes

These fishes, forming the family Diodontidae, are also able to inflate themselves. The mouth is again small, but with a powerful bite. The eyes protrude and can be turned in all directions, thus giving the fish a very wide visual field so

Diodon hystrix

small pieces of mussel or fish flesh, but they should not of course be kept in a tank with invertebrates, which they will soon consume.

Suitable species for the aquarium include *Arothron hispidus* (50 cm or $19\frac{1}{2}$ in) and *A. nigropunctatus* (25 cm or $9\frac{3}{4}$ in) both from the Indo-Pacific area. Some of the smaller species with pointed heads are perhaps more suitable for the home aquarium, although these too will attack any invertebrates. They belong to the subfamily Canthigasterinae, and include *Canthigaster margaritatus* (15 cm or 6 in) and the related *C. valentini* (20 cm or $7\frac{3}{4}$ in), both from the Indo-Pacific area.

that it can retreat to a sheltered spot among the rocks or corals when threatened. On the reefs these strange fishes often live in association with soldierfishes. Porcupinefishes frequently kept include *Chilomycterus schoepfi* (25 cm or $9\frac{3}{4}$ in) from the western Atlantic (Cape Cod to Rio de Janeiro), and *Diodon holacanthus* (50 cm or $19\frac{1}{2}$ in) and *D. hystrix* (86 cm or 35 in), both from tropical seas.

Invertebrates for the marine aquarium

Marine invertebrates are considerably more sensitive to the quality of the water than the true fishes. As the name implies, these animals, unlike the vertebrates (fishes, amphibians, reptiles, birds and mammals), do not have a vertebral column. Some invertebrates do, however, have an external hard skeleton or shell, e.g. crustaceans, snails, bivalves, sea-urchins.

The principal groups of marine invertebrates are the coelenterates (sea-anemones, jellyfishes, corals), the sponges, the molluscs (gastropods or snails, bivalves and octopuses), the worms (bristle-worms, tubeworms) and the echinoderms (starfishes, brittlestars, sea-urchins, sea-cucumbers, feather-stars). Many of these can be kept in the aquarium but they are not all easy to maintain.

Sponges

A sponge is made up of very large numbers of microscopic cells which are adapted for taking in sea water and filtering minute food particles from it. Suitable food of this type is not usually present in an aquarium, so sponges are not to be recommended except for the very experienced. If they are kept they should be placed in a dimly lit corner of the tank, as they will soon die if algae start to grow on their surface.

Coelenterates

The basic structure of a coelenterate is a hollow sac open at the top end where the mouth is surrounded by rings of tentacles. Prey is caught by sting cells on the tentacles and passed into the mouth, and thence into the hollow sac or enteron where it is digested. Jellyfishes are not suitable for the aquarium, but various kinds of sea-anemones can be kept successfully, and occasionally small pieces of live coral.

Sea-anemones are found in all tropical and subtropical seas, and there are also numerous species on the shores in temperate regions. Most

An orange-red sponge

Variously coloured ceriantharians, with a starfish *(Protoreaster lincki)*

A sea-anemone *(Radianthus)* with a symbiotic prawn *(Periclimenes)*

of the types kept in marine aquarium tanks come from tropical waters where some of them grow to over three feet in diameter. For the home aquarium they would need to be much smaller than this.

The association of anemone-fishes (genus *Amphiprion*) with large sea-anemones has already been mentioned. Under aquarium conditions it seems that the anemones usually get the worst of the bargain. They require a plentiful supply of oxygen and a fast water circulation. They should not, however, be put immediately in front of the water inlet, but should be sheltered from the direct current by a suitably placed rock.

If they do not feel 'comfortable', sea-anemones tend to wander about the tank and this may be annoying.

The sea-anemones of the order Ceriantharia live with the body buried in the sand or gravel. They emerge and unfold their beautiful, delicate tentacles when conditions in the tank are to their liking, but will immediately withdraw and become invisible if disturbed. They are not particularly difficult to feed, for they will take small pieces of mussel flesh or freeze-dried prawns which can be merely dropped onto the crown of tentacles. These attractive sea-anemones occur in several colour variants and they are well worth keeping.

The anemones that live in association with anemone-fishes mostly belong to the genera *Stoichactis* and *Discosoma*, but they are primarily plankton-feeders so they rarely get enough food in the aquarium and gradually become smaller and smaller, and finally die. The related anemone genus *Radianthus* has some species which appear to do better in captivity, particularly the one from the Caribbean area, known in the aquarium trade as the Florida anemone. It is interesting that these Caribbean anemones will accept the presence of the fishes even though there are no anemone-fishes in their home waters (all species of *Amphiprion* and related genera are restricted to the Indo-Pacific).

A bivalve mollusc *(Lima* sp.*)*   Sea-urchin *(Tripneustes gratilla)*

White-banded cleaner prawn   Red hermit-crab *(Dardanus megistos)*

Gorgonians

Most aquarists will know the gorgonians from their very decorative horny skeletons which show traces of the numerous small polyps, for gorgonians are colonial coelenterates which live attached to rocks in areas where brisk currents bring them the plankton on which they feed. Live gorgonians can be kept in a marine tank, provided the water circulation is really efficient and as long as algae are not allowed to grow on them.

Molluscs

The phylum Mollusca is one of the major groups of the animal kingdom. It is made up of a number of classes, the most important of which are the gastropods (snails, slugs), the bivalves (mussels, oysters, clams) and the cephalopods (squids, cuttlefishes and octopuses). Many species of gastropods and bivalves are imported from tropical seas and some live quite well in marine tanks. Among the gastropods there are several species of the very attractive cowries, such as the tiger cowry *Cypraea tigris* and the related *C. mappa* and *C. mauritiana*. Only small specimens should be used, and in a well-established tank they will find their own food, browsing algae from the rocks and picking up scraps of food left by other animals. The genus *Murex* also has species that do well, although they are mainly active at night. These gastropods are, however, predators and they will attack and eat other animals such as worms and sea-urchins. Another gastropod sometimes imported is *Mitra papalis*.

The cone shells of the family Conidae are sometimes to be found on the market, but they are extremely dangerous animals to have in a tank. They produce a venom which they inject into their prey. A small fish attacked by a cone shell dies immediately, and the aquarist's fingers are also at risk.

Bivalve molluscs are interesting to keep, although not many can be said to be attractive. The two valves of the shell are joined by a hinge, and they can be tightly closed by the contraction of a powerful muscle. Bivalves in which this muscle is not functioning should not be bought, as they will certainly die in quite a short time and the decay of their soft parts will pollute the tank water. Bivalves frequently imported include *Lima scabra* and small specimens of *Tridacna*, the genus containing the giant clams of the Indo-Pacific. These are, however, plankton

A tiger cowrie *(Cypraea tigris)* showing (left) the shell completely covered by the mantle, and (right) the shell partially exposed by the withdrawal of the mantle

feeders and can take only very small particles. Larger particles are rejected long before they reach the alimentary canal. The *Tridacna* species have algal cells, known as zooxanthellae, living in their tissues. These cells need light, and in nature they receive plenty because the clams always live in shallow water. In the aquarium they should be placed so as to receive the maximum amount of light. Even so they do not usually survive for long in the home aquarium.

An attractive group of corals and small tubeworms

Worms

The worms of the phylum Annelida form another large animal group. Apart from the earthworms and leeches, which do not concern us here, the group also contains the bristle-worms or Polychaeta, and some of these are very attractive in a marine tank. The types usually kept are those that live in tubes of their own making. Such tubeworms, belonging to the families Serpulidae, Sabellidae and Terebellidae, are usually imported attached to pieces of rock, where they may be living alongside other sessile animals, such as corals and sponges. Some tubeworms construct their tube out of sand particles cemented by a slimy secretion; others make a calcareous tube which is, of course, more resistant. Empty calcareous tubes of this type are common objects of the seashore in all parts of the world. The worms living in these tubes expand their beautiful tentacles to catch food particles, but if disturbed they can withdraw the whole crown of tentacles in a fraction of a second. In a healthy tubeworm only the tentacles will be visible, but if the whole body comes out of the tube it is a sign that the worm is going to die. In most tanks there will be enough suspended particulate matter to feed a few tubeworms.

Crustaceans

The class Crustacea contains a wide variety of animals, ranging in size from tiny water-fleas to giant crabs. Some crustaceans live on land, but the vast majority are aquatic, and particularly abundant in the sea. Several crustaceans of the group Decapoda can be kept in the aquarium. Larger decapods such as lobsters and crawfishes are only suitable for the very large tanks in a public aquarium, but many of the much smaller shrimps and prawns do very well in the home aquarium. One of the best of these is *Stenopus hispidus*, which has an attractive pattern and has been seen to clean scraps of skin from fishes. During the day it usually lives hidden away under a piece of rock or coral. This species can be kept as a true pair, but two of the same sex will quarrel and, within the confines of a tank, the weaker may be unable to escape and may be killed. Such small crustaceans do not need to be specially fed, as they live perfectly well on the scraps left by the fishes.

Some of the prawns live in association with sea-anemones, a phenomenon known in scientific terms as symbiosis. Two species that live in this way are *Periclimenes brevicarpalis* and *P. pedersoni*. On the other hand the little harlequin prawn, *Hymenocera picta*, has very different habits, for it feeds mainly on starfishes. Often working with a partner of the same species, it is able to turn over a starfish and then gradually eat it.

Cleaner prawn, *Stenopus hispidus*

The predatory prawn *Hymenocera picta* eating a starfish *Protoreaster lincki*

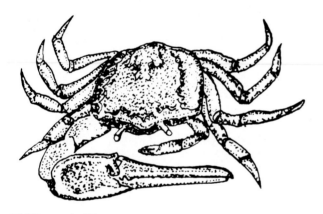

Fiddler crab, *Uca* sp.

Tropical hermit-crabs are frequently available on the market. These, too, are decapod crustaceans but they live with the soft, rear part of their body tucked into an empty gastropod shell. As they grow they have to change their shell for a larger size, so a tank containing hermit-crabs should have a selection of empty shells of various sizes. Empty *Murex* shells are particularly suitable. Unfortunately, hermit-crabs are very predatory and so are quite unsuitable for a tank containing invertebrates. The red hermit-crab, *Dardanus megistos*, is an attractive species often imported.

Some of the small crabs imported from tropical shores are also suitable for the aquarium. Many of these spend part of their time out of the water, and they can therefore be kept in a tank with shallow water, with a few rocks sticking up out of the water and a tiny beach of sand or gravel where the crabs can come out at will. Among these are the well-known fiddler-crabs of the genus *Uca* in which the male has a particularly large pincer on one side.

Echinoderms

These are the starfishes, brittlestars, sea-urchins, sea-cucumbers and feather-stars which are exclusively marine animals forming the phylum Echinodermata. Starfishes of various kinds do quite well provided they have not suffered injury during collection and transit. They move about with the help of hydraulically operated tubefeet, each of which has a small sucker at the end. These enable them to climb vertical surfaces underwater. They should never be roughly removed from a rock or the aquarium glass, as this would injure the attached tubefeet. Starfishes are, in general, predatory animals. Those with broad arms, such as *Oreaster*, *Pentaceraster* and *Protoreaster* are usually more active predators than those with round arms, such as the blue starfish *Linckia laevigata*, and various species of *Echinaster*, *Leiaster* and *Ophidiaster*. On the whole, *Linckia* is probably the most suitable tropical starfish for an aquarium tank.

Sea-urchins are not so easy to keep as they are rather more sensitive to the quality of the water, and they also require a supply of algae to feed on. They move about in the same way as starfishes, but their tubefeet are longer, having to extend

A feather-star which, like the sea-cucumbers, belongs among the echinoderms

top and above: a sea-cucumber or holothurian, two views to show the attractive crown of tentacles

A tropical sea-urchin *(Diadema)*

Orange and blue sponges with a red sea-urchin

beyond the spines. In a sea-urchin not in healthy condition the spines will tend to droop, whereas in a healthy specimen they are held erect. If the spines are shed the sea-urchin is more or less moribund, and should be immediately removed from the tank. Sea-urchins with very long spines are not often imported. They are difficult to transport as their spines soon puncture the usual plastic bags used for transporting marine animals. The spines are also very brittle, and in many species they carry poison at the tips, so great care must be taken when handling them. An attractive sea-urchin with short spines is *Toxopneustes gratilla* which not only feeds on algae, but also uses them as camouflage by attaching bunches to the tubefeet on its upper surface. The small, oval sea-urchins of the genus *Echinometra* also come from tropical seas, and they live quite well in the aquarium. The usual species imported are *Echinometra mathaei* (reddish-violet) from the Indo-Pacific and *E. lucunter* (pale grey).

Index

Page numbers in italic refer to illustrations

Index of plants

Index of fishes and invertebrates